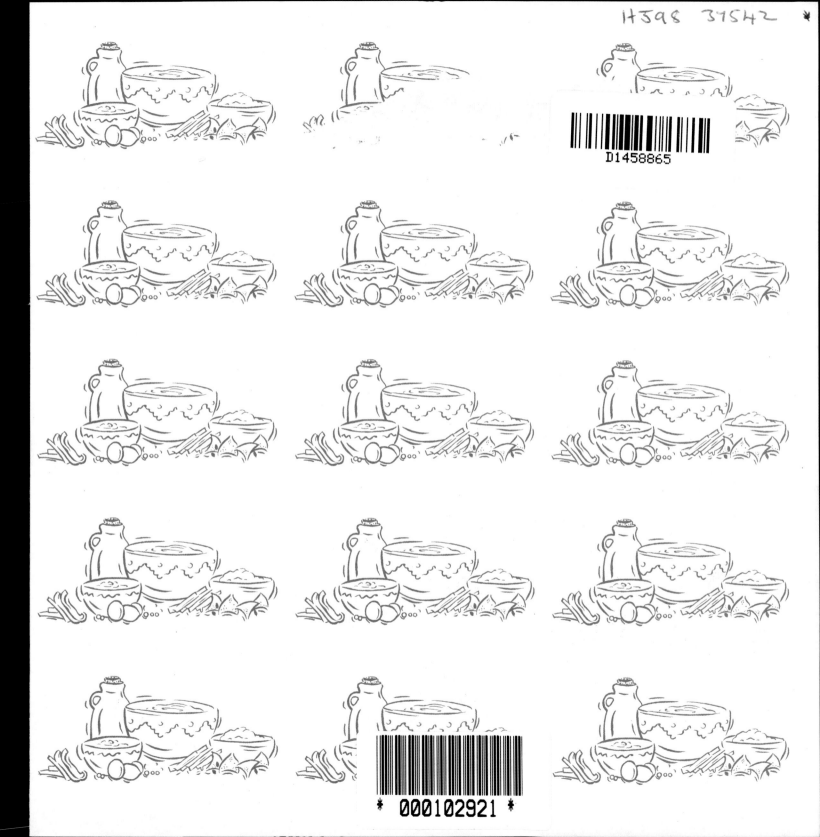

ONE HUNDRED
HUNDRED
HOME-MADE
DIPS

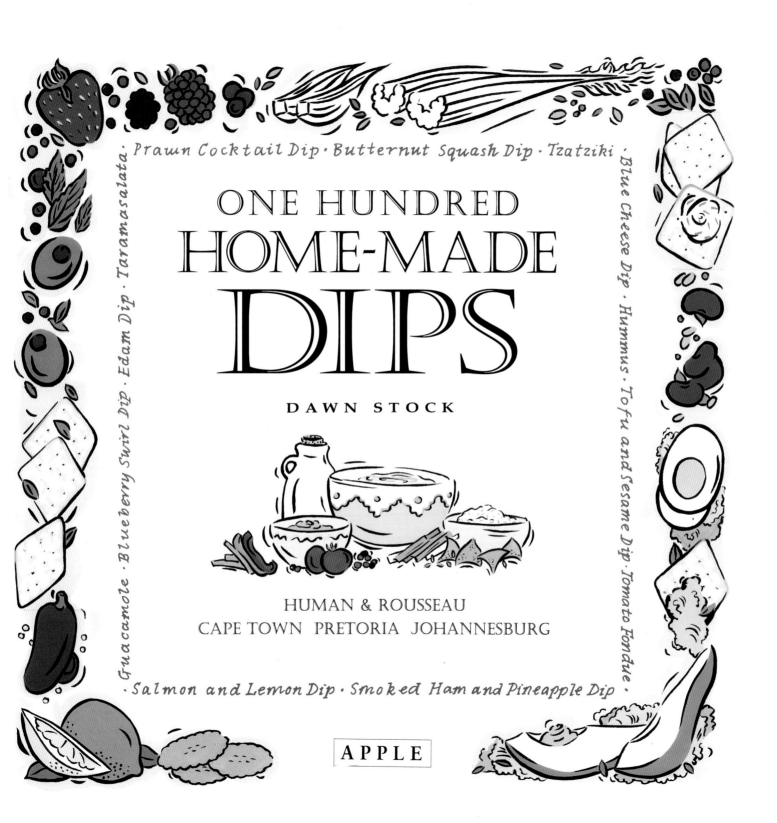

Prawn Cocktail Dip · Butternut Squash Dip · Tzatziki

ONE HUNDRED
HOME-MADE
DIPS

DAWN STOCK

HUMAN & ROUSSEAU
CAPE TOWN PRETORIA JOHANNESBURG

Taramasalata · Edam Dip · Blueberry Swirl Dip · Guacamole

Blue Cheese Dip · Hummus · Tofu and Sesame Dip · Tomato Fondue

· Salmon and Lemon Dip · Smoked Ham and Pineapple Dip ·

APPLE

A QUINTET BOOK

Published by Apple Press
6 Blundell Street
London N7 9BH

ISBN 1-85076-717-3

This book was designed and produced by
Quintet Publishing Limited
6 Blundell Street
London N7 9BH

Creative Director: Richard Dewing
Designer: Ian Hunt
Project Editor: Diana Steedman
Editor: Amy Boaz Nugent
Illustrator: Joanne Makin

Typeset in Great Britain by
Central Southern Typesetters, Eastbourne
Manufactured in Singapore by
Universal Graphics Pte Ltd
Printed in Singapore by
Star Standard Industries (Pte) Ltd

Contents

INTRODUCTION 6

CHAPTER ONE CHEESE DIPS 12

CHAPTER TWO FISH DIPS 19

CHAPTER THREE POULTRY AND MEAT DIPS 26

CHAPTER FOUR VEGETABLE DIPS 33

CHAPTER FIVE BEAN AND LENTIL DIPS 46

CHAPTER SIX FRUIT DIPS – SAVOURY AND SWEET 51

CHAPTER SEVEN FONDUES 59

CHAPTER EIGHT MORE FAVOURITES 64

CHAPTER NINE WHAT GOES WITH WHAT 70

INDEX 80

Introduction

This collection of recipes was put together with a lot of enjoyment since all of the different dips tested and devised have such a wide variety of flavours and textures there was never a chance for the taste buds to get bored. The majority of dips included here are very quick and easy to make, which make them ideal foods for the trend towards snacking rather than eating set meals. However, this is not an endorsement of the "grazing" style of eating, and I still believe that taking time out to sit down and enjoy good food and company properly makes us happier and healthier folk.

The cookbook is conveniently divided into eight, covering the different dips: cheese, fish, poultry and meat, vegetables, bean and lentil, fruit (savoury and sweet), fondues (savory and sweet), and more favourites with a final section containing "at a glance" tables of all 100 dips and their serving suggestions that you can browse through (or maybe even dip into) for inspiration.

But first, before you start cooking, here's just a few words about the various types of dips included, a few helpful preparation and serving tips, some ideas and hints on preparing the accompaniments, and the cook's notes to help make your life in the kitchen easier.

TYPES OF DIPS

There is certainly more to the culinary world of dips than just a bowl of chilled yogurt and a few strips of raw vegetables, and that's without starting to think about all the different types of foods which can be served with a dip. Dips can be savoury or sweet, cooked or uncooked, served hot or cold. Many consider the fondue the ultimate dip. You'll learn more about fondue techniques at the beginning of the fondue chapter. Throughout the book, you will find dips covering all the above possibilities.

Dips are no new thing; we have probably been dipping into our foods since we evolved. In the early days, when there were no plates or eating implements, what better way of scooping up your food than with other vegetables, fruits and bread. Throughout the world, there are national favourite dips and this book includes a selection of the most popular and well known, such as hummus and tzatziki from Greece, guacamole from Mexico, tapenade from Spain, raita and dhals from India, and dips from China and Thailand.

The popularity of dips may be due to the fact that there is something satisfying and familiar about dipping your finger into a sauce when cooking, or, when we were younger, being allowed to clean out the chocolate icing bowl. Maybe dips are an adult way in which we can indulge ourselves in this satisfying way of eating.

WHEN TO SERVE DIPS

Dips tend to be an informal way of eating, which in itself adds to their enjoyment and makes them ideal for serving to family and friends, or even as a treat when by yourself. Most of us probably think of serving dips at parties or as a first course at a dinner; however, dips can be served at any time of the day, from a wholesome brunch (see Creamy Egg Brunch Dip, page 68 – ideal for when you have guests for the weekend or at a working breakfast), to snacks any time of the day, light lunches, and packed lunches, first courses, main meals, desserts, suppers, at parties and when entertaining (see Scarlet Delight Dip for Halloween, page 35, and Cranberry and Orange Dip for serving at Thanksgiving or Christmas, page 52). We don't need an excuse when to dip – we can treat ourselves any time, even when watching television or reading.

HOW TO SERVE DIPS

No strict rules apply as to how to serve dips, since they tend to be informal and generally need no special serving equipment. Special fondue sets and forks can be purchased, which add fun to the occasion, but I find keeping the fondue warm on a tabletop warmer with nightlights just as effective.

All you need is a suitable serving bowl to serve the dip in, or individual ramekin dishes and plates or bowls in which to arrange the variety of dipping accompaniments. Unusual containers in which to serve your dip can liven up your table setting. Hollow out a crusty loaf or individual bread rolls to make an unusual, edible bowl. Fruits and vegetables can also be hollowed out and filled with a dip. Pineapples, large tomatoes, aubergines, peppers and squash all make great serving containers. A crab dip looks stunning if served in cleaned crab shells.

PREPARATION IN ADVANCE

Many dips actually benefit from being made well in advance so that they have several hours chilling time in order for the flavours to mingle and mature. The exceptions tend to be dips made with fresh fruit which exude natural juices, making the dip too moist if chilled for too long, and fondues which are best made and served immediately. If a dip benefits from several hours chilling time or requires serving soon after being made, a recommendation has been made in that particular recipe.

The consistency of the dips throughout the book vary greatly, from fairly thin to a thick and hearty spread. Some are smooth, others crunchy, and the salsas are made from small diced vegetables and fruits that require substantial accompaniments with which to scoop up the chunky pieces.

Dips made with cream cheese, soured cream and yogurt tend to thicken upon chilling, so before serving, stir the dip to soften its texture sufficiently. However, if you find your dip still a little too thick, simply stir in one to two tablespoons of milk before transferring it to a serving dish.

Many vegetables used as raw dipping accompaniments can be prepared several hours in advance, then placed in an airtight container and kept in the refrigerator. Carrots, celery, courgettes, cucumber, crisp lettuce leaves, broccoli and cauliflower florets, strips of colourful peppers, trimmed spring onions, fennel and endive are all suitable for advance preparation. However, quartered button mushrooms are best prepared just before serving to prevent discolouration, tomato wedges become too wet if left to stand in their own juices, and onion wedges and rings are best prepared just prior to serving because their strong odour may taint other foods.

Some vegetables are better used for dipping after they have been cooked very slightly. These can be prepared well in advance, drained, and left to chill in the refrigerator. Baby sweet corn, green beans, mange tout and asparagus tips are particularly good once cooked and chilled. The cooking time entails little more than blanching. Trim the vegetables if necessary and bring a pan of water to the boil. Add the vegetables, return the pan to the boil, and simmer for no more than one to two minutes so that the vegetables are still crunchy. Drain in a colander and cool with cold running water and drain well.

Deep-fried, batter-coated vegetables can be partially prepared in advance. The batter (see page 28 for recipe) can be made and chilled until required and the vegetables chopped into bite-sized pieces and chilled in an airtight container until they need coating and cooking.

Fruits used for dipping are best prepared not too far in advance because they can become wet if left in their own juices. Some fruits, for example apple, pears, bananas and peaches, discolour when cut open. To help prevent fruit from discolouring and browning, the fruit can be dipped in lemon, lime or orange juice immediately after slicing and then arranged on a serving plate.

THINGS FOR DIPPING

It is important to stress that you need to use the best quality and freshest produce available. There is nothing worse than trying to scoop up a dip with a limp piece of carrot or lettuce leaf past its prime. Vegetables should be crisp and crunchy with a fresh colour, while fruits should be ripe, but not overripe and certainly not bruised. Even if the vegetables and fruits are to be served barbecued, grilled, or batter-coated and fried, they still need to be of the best quality.

Many vegetables tend to be cut into strips, called sticks or crudités. Don't make the strips too long or else you end up with too much vegetable and too little dip, and there's a temptation to redip after you've taken a bite. Too short and the vegetable, and your fingers, get covered in dip as you scoop. Both of these are no problem if you're eating by yourself, but may not impress your guests. I find cutting the vegetable strips to about 5 cm (2 in) long ideal.

Pears, apples, peaches, nectarines, paw-paw, mango and melons are best served in small wedges, with their skins removed, cored or deseeded as required. Bananas can be served in sticks and soft fruits such as seedless grapes, strawberries and raspberries can be hulled and left whole. You may find it helpful to use small forks or cocktail sticks for picking up the fruit and dipping.

Fish, meat and poultry can be served cut into bite-sized nuggets. Strips of batter- or crumb-coated fish, meat and poultry are also sometimes called *goujons*, which adds a certain classiness to your dip, particularly if you're entertaining to impress. Use tender and lean cuts that will stay tender after quick cooking, as grilling, stir frying and deep frying are ideal cooking methods for fast accompaniments to dips.

Many batter- or crumb-coated bite-sized meat and poultry products now exist in the supermarkets and make fine accompaniments to dips. However, it can be fun to make your own individual accompaniments and you can refer to the batter- and crumb-coated turkey recipes on page 28 and 52. These coatings can also be used with other meats or fish and the batter used on vegetables and fruits as well.

There are many other foods suitable for dipping, see the charts on pages 70–79, plus you will have your own personal discoveries. However, below are a few more ideas to spark your imagination and taste buds.

The ever-increasing selection of breads available from bakeries and supermarkets make ideal accompaniments – they are economical, tasty and filling. They are also easy to prepare, requiring only to be sliced or cubed. Bread can also be toasted, made into croutons, garlic bread and melba toast. Don't forget the special breads as well, such as pitta, bagels and flavoured breads such as olive, tomato, rye and pumpernickel.

Breadsticks, crackers, potato crisps, tortilla crisps, nachos, prawn and rice crackers all add different tastes and textures to the meal as accompaniments to dips.

And for those with a sweet tooth, you'll find it hard to resist the selection of sweet fondues and fruit dips. Dipping marshmallows, biscuits, mini doughnuts and cubed cake into Autumnal Fruits with Port Dip or Devil's Chocolate Fondue is simply delicious.

ARE DIPS HEALTHY?

As with most things – there is the good and the bad! Some dips can be considered extremely healthy, low in calories, fat, sugar and salt, while others are laden with fat, sugar and calories. However, this book contains a selection of both so there should be something to suit everyone's diet and lifestyle.

Some of the dips could be considered very righteous because they are low in fat and salt and when served with plenty of raw vegetables or fruit and crusty bread make a nutritious snack or meal. Others can be made "healthier" for those of you counting the calories or fat content by using the lower fat alternatives such as low fat/reduced calorie mayonnaise, yogurt or cream cheese. However, some of the dips were just meant to be rich and there's no reason why most of us shouldn't treat ourselves occasionally.

Remember, it's not just the dips that should be considered, it's often the foods we choose to dip them with that can make the most difference. Choose healthier dipping options such as raw fruit and vegetables, delicious by themselves, rather than the batter-coated and fried varieties. Use fruit instead of cakes, biscuits and marshmallows. A selection of cubed crusty brown and white breads are delicious and filling and healthier than dipping crisps and other salty fried snack foods.

But most important, if possible don't just snatch a meal or snack: these dips are quick and easy to prepare so take a little time out to enjoy some good food either by yourself or in the company of family and friends.

10

HOW MANY PEOPLE DO THE DIPS SERVE?

Portions depend on when and how you intend to serve the dip. If you are serving the dip at a buffet party with lots of other foods, then the dip will serve considerably more than when eaten by itself. I find it is better to serve several different dips at a buffet rather than making vast quantities of just one dip. Make sure you have plenty of dipping accompaniments nearby.

However, as a general guideline the dips that make 300–375 ml/10–12 fl oz will serve about four to six people as a starter or first course and about two to three people as a main course when served with plenty of dipping accompaniments.

The dips that make 450–600 ml/15–20 fl oz will serve about eight to twelve as a starter and four to six people as a main meal.

A little of your own judgment and knowing your guest's appetites will help determine serving quantities and how much food you will need as dipping accompaniments. I have always found that it is best to provide more than you think you'll need, particularly with fondues, since there is a great temptation when sitting and chatting to dip and dip, again and again!

COOK'S NOTES

Please take a few moments to read these notes before starting to make any of the recipes.

1. The quantities made by the dips are approximate guidelines and are given to help you assess how much you will make and how many people it will serve to suit your requirements.

2. Cooking times are given as a guideline, but may vary with different ovens. Helpful hints on what to look for at the cooked stage have been given in the recipes to ensure you get the best results.

3. All spoon measurements are level spoonfuls.

4. All eggs used are medium-sized eggs.

5. Freshly ground black pepper has been used to season many of the dips. Salt has rarely been added, but do season to your own taste.

6. Some of the recipes require the chopping and deseeding of fresh chillies. If you are unfamiliar with handling chillies, take care to wash your hands and utensils thoroughly after cutting them. If you prefer a hot chilli flavour there is no need to remove the seeds since they contain a lot of the chilli's fiery heat.

7. The Garlic Dip and Creamy Egg Brunch Dip contain raw or soft-boiled eggs. Note that eggs should not be consumed raw or lightly cooked by people at risk, such as those with weak immune systems and pregnant women. The other recipes use hard-boiled eggs, which are fully cooked and can be safely consumed by those considered at risk.

8. The ingredients used in the dips need to be stored in the refrigerator for safety and hygiene. Where the recipes say chill, it is important to use the refrigerator for this purpose.

CHEESE
DIPS

4

Ricotta and Cream Walnut Dip

MAKES ABOUT 375 ML/12 FL OZ

The Italian cheese Ricotta has a very mild, smooth, creamy flavour, so the pieces of walnut add a crunchy bite.

250 g/9 oz Ricotta
5 Tbsp double cream
125 g/4 oz shelled walnuts, chopped
4 Tbsp fresh parsley, chopped
Freshly ground black pepper
Strips of celery, apple wedges and bagels

1. Soften the Ricotta with the double cream in a bowl until smooth and well combined.
2. Stir the chopped walnuts into the dip, reserving a few for garnish. Add the parsley. Season to taste with freshly ground black pepper. Cover and chill.
3. Turn the dip into a serving bowl and garnish with the reserved walnuts. Serve with celery sticks, cored apple wedges (dipped in lemon juice to prevent discolouring) and bagels cut into bite-sized pieces.

Beer and Cheddar Dip

MAKES ABOUT 375 ML/12 FL OZ

A "ploughman's lunch" all in a dip! Use a strong-flavoured cheddar to complement the beer.

125 g/4 oz strong cheddar cheese, finely grated
200 g/7 oz cream cheese
75 ml/3 fl oz beer
Freshly ground black pepper
Trimmed spring onions, crisps and breadsticks

1. Soften the cream cheese in a bowl and stir in the cheddar.
2. Gradually blend in the beer and season the dip with freshly ground black pepper. Cover and chill.
3. Transfer the dip to a serving bowl. Serve with spring onions, crisps and breadsticks.

Green Olive and Cream Cheese Dip

MAKES ABOUT 450 ML/15 FL OZ

This hearty dip is ripe with flavour and quite a feast when served with breadsticks and warmed strips of pitta bread.

200 g/7 oz low-fat cream cheese
50 g/2 oz low-calorie mayonnaise
200 g/7 oz pitted green olives
2 spring onions, finely chopped
Freshly ground black pepper
Breadsticks and pitta bread, cut into strips

1. Blend the cream cheese and mayonnaise in a mixing bowl.
2. Reserve five olives for a garnish and place the remaining olives in a small blender and process for a few seconds until chopped but not completely smooth.
3. Add the processed olives and chopped spring onions to the cheese mixture and mix thoroughly. Season to taste with freshly ground black pepper. Spoon into a serving dish and garnish with olive rings cut from the reserved olives. Cover and chill.
4. Serve with breadsticks and strips of warmed pitta bread.

Cheese and Pimento Dip

MAKES ABOUT 300 ML/10 FL OZ

If possible, use freshly grated Parmesan rather than the ready-grated variety for a full-flavoured dip.

50 g/2 oz Parmesan, finely grated
50 g/2 oz strong cheddar cheese, finely grated
250 g/9 oz drained canned pimentoes
A few drops of chilli sauce
Breadsticks and potato and tortilla crisps

1. Mix together the Parmesan and cheddar cheeses in a bowl.
2. Place the pimentoes in a blender or food processor and process for a few seconds until smooth. Mix the puréed pimentoes with the cheese and season to taste with a few drops of chilli sauce. Cover and chill.
3. Transfer the dip to a serving bowl and serve with breadsticks and potato and tortilla crisps.

Brie and Pear Dip

MAKES ABOUT 375 ML/12 FL OZ

This dip is best served fairly soon after making in order to enjoy the flavour of the pear. It becomes masked by the brie on keeping.

1 ripe pear
125 g/4 oz natural fromage frais
150 g/5 oz brie cheese
Freshly ground black pepper
Small wedges of cantaloupe and watermelon, skin and seeds removed

1. Peel and core the pear. Chop coarsely and place in a blender or food processor with the fromage frais. Process for a few seconds until smooth.
2. Add the brie in chunks and process until smooth. Season well with freshly ground black pepper. Place in a serving dish, cover and chill.
3. Serve the dip with small wedges of cantaloupe and watermelon.

Pistachio and Blue Cheese Dip

MAKES ABOUT 300 ML/10 FL OZ

Simply delicious is the verdict for this dip and a firm favourite in my house. The pistachios add a wonderful crunchy texture to the creamy rich dip.

125 g/4 oz blue cheese
150 g/5 oz fromage frais
3 Tbsp milk
75 g/3 oz pistachios, roasted in their shells
Freshly ground black pepper
Crusty bread, strips of celery and wedges of crisp apple

1. Crumble the blue cheese finely into a bowl with the back of a fork.
2. Stir in the fromage frais and enough milk to make a coating dip. Mix well.
3. Shell the pistachios and rub off any excess husk and skin where possible. Coarsely chop the nuts, reserving a few for garnish. Stir the chopped pistachios into the dip, cover and chill.
4. Spoon the dip into a serving dish and garnish with the reserved chopped pistachios. Serve with small chunks of crusty bread, strips of celery and cored apple wedges (dipped in lemon juice to prevent discolouring).

Smoked Cheese Dip

MAKES ABOUT 300 ML/10 FL OZ

The smoked flavour matures and gets stronger the longer this dip is chilled.

150 g/5 oz smoked processed cheese
200 g/7 oz mayonnaise
1 tsp Dijon mustard
Freshly ground black pepper
Toasted cubes of bread, a selection of crackers, tomato wedges and cucumber strips

1. Break the cheese into chunks and place in a blender or food processor with the mayonnaise and mustard. Process for a few seconds until smooth.
2. Spoon into a bowl and season with freshly ground black pepper. Cover and chill.
3. Transfer the dip to a serving bowl. Serve with toasted cubes of bread, a selection of crackers, tomato wedges and strips of cucumber.

Dill, Yogurt and Cream Cheese Dip

MAKES ABOUT 300 ML/10 FL OZ

The sweet, slightly aniseed flavour of dill makes this dip a wonderful accompaniment to fennel, endive and cucumber crudités.

200 g/7 oz low-fat cream cheese
150 g/5 oz low-fat natural yogurt
3 Tbsp fresh dill, chopped
1 tsp lemon juice
Freshly ground black pepper
Fresh dill sprigs
Lemon slices
Strips of fennel, endive and cucumber

1. Soften the cream cheese in a mixing bowl with a spoon. Blend in the yogurt to form a smooth consistency.
2. Stir the chopped dill into the yogurt mixture along with the lemon juice.
3. Season to taste with freshly ground black pepper. Cover and chill.
4. To serve, transfer the dip to a serving bowl, garnish with dill sprigs and slices of lemon. Serve with vegetable crudités of fennel, endive and cucumber. This dip is also well suited to serve with deep-fried batter- or crumb-coated strips of fish.

Peppercorn Cheese Dip

MAKES ABOUT 300 ML/10 FL OZ

If possible, use mixed white, green and black peppercorns for varying colours and strengths to add flavour and interest to the dip. Use freshly grated Parmesan, not the ready-grated variety available at the supermarket – the flavour is 100 times superior.

200 g/7 oz cream cheese
4 Tbsp Parmesan, finely grated
4 Tbsp milk
3 Tbsp mixed whole peppercorns (white, green and black)
Breadsticks, cheese straws, strips of cucumber and carrot

1. Soften the cream cheese in a bowl and stir in the Parmesan.
2. Add the milk gradually to the cheese mixture to make a smooth dip.
3. Lightly crush the peppercorns in a pestle and mortar. Alternatively place the peppercorns in a small plastic bag and gently roll a rolling pin over the bag to crush the peppercorns. Take care not to overcrush the peppercorns since it is best if the dip has a slightly crunchy texture.
4. Stir the peppercorns into the cheese dip mixture, cover and chill.
5. Spoon the dip into a serving dish and serve with breadsticks, cheese straws and strips of cucumber and carrot.

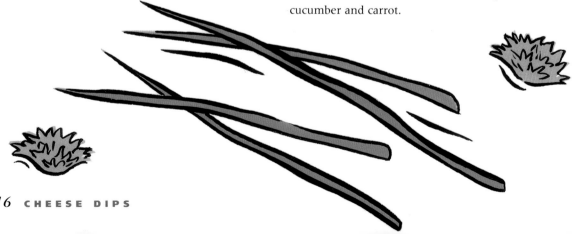

Mountain High Dip

MAKES ABOUT 375 ML/12 FL OZ

150 g/5 oz goat's cheese
150 g/5 oz double cream
25 g/1 oz mixed herbs (e.g. parsley, chives, oregano, thyme)
Freshly ground black pepper
Chunks of crusty bread and hearty strips of celery,
cucumber and carrot

1. Soften the goat's cheese in a bowl with the back of a fork.
2. In a separate bowl, lightly whip the cream to a soft, dropping consistency.
3. Remove any large or woody stalks from the herbs and chop the leaves very finely. Mix the cream and herbs into the softened goat's cheese. Season to taste with freshly ground black pepper. Cover and chill.
4. Spoon the dip into a serving dish and serve with chunky pieces of crusty bread and hearty strips of celery, cucumber and carrot.

Cream Cheese and Chive Dip

MAKES ABOUT 300 ML/10 FL OZ

Delicate chives are more subtle in flavour than raw onion and using low-calorie alternatives helps make this dip a healthier option for those of you watching your fat intake or counting calories.

200 g/7 oz low-fat cream cheese
3 Tbsp low-calorie mayonnaise
4 Tbsp skimmed milk
1 tsp Dijon mustard
3 Tbsp fresh chives, chopped
Freshly ground black pepper
Fresh chive flowers (if in season)
Red onion wedges, celery, carrot, pepper strips

1. Soften cream cheese in a mixing bowl with the mayonnaise and milk until smooth.
2. Stir in the mustard and chives, reserving some for garnish. Season to taste with freshly ground black pepper. Cover and chill.
3. To serve, spoon into a serving bowl and garnish with remaining chopped chives or chive flowers. Serve with red onion wedges and strips of celery, carrot and peppers.

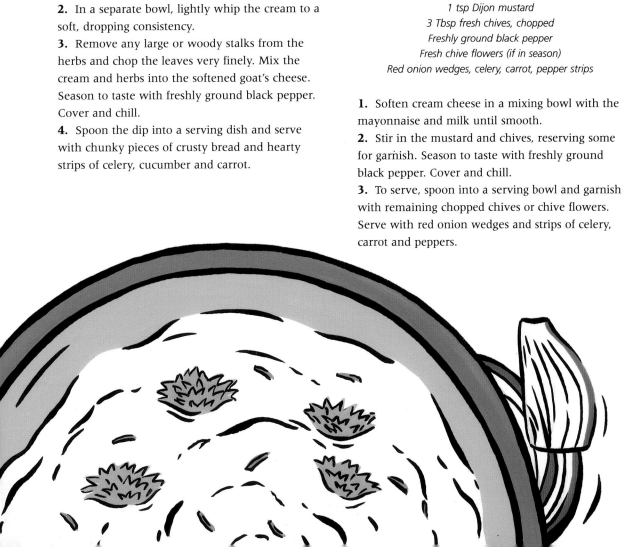

Blue Cheese Dip

MAKES ABOUT 450 ML/15 FL OZ

This dip can take strong-flavoured crudités such
as cauliflower and broccoli. The longer it chills
in the refrigerator, the more the flavour develops.

150 g/5 oz strong blue cheese, e.g. Danish Blue
300 ml/10 fl oz soured cream
2 Tbsp celery leaves, finely chopped
Freshly ground black pepper
Strips of celery and small florets of cauliflower and broccoli
Celery leaves to garnish

1. Crumble the blue cheese finely into a mixing
bowl with a fork.
2. Add the soured cream and celery leaves
reserving some leaves for garnish. Mix thoroughly.
Season to taste with freshly ground black pepper.
Cover and chill.
3. To serve, turn the dip into a serving bowl and
garnish with celery leaves. Serve with raw strips of
celery and small florets of cauliflower and broccoli.

Edam Dip

MAKES ABOUT 300 ML/10 FL OZ

If you can find a small whole Edam, carefully
cut off the top and hollow out the cheese so
that it can then be used as a container in which
to serve your dip.

125 g/4 oz Edam, finely grated
150 g/5 oz natural low-fat yogurt
3 Tbsp low-calorie mayonnaise
2 pinches of paprika
Freshly ground black pepper
Quartered button mushrooms, tomato wedges, broccoli
florets and sticks of carrot

1. Mix the grated Edam with the yogurt and
mayonnaise in a bowl.
2. Add a pinch of paprika and season well with
freshly ground black pepper. Cover and chill.
3. Spoon the dip into a serving bowl or hollowed
cheese and sprinkle with a pinch of paprika to
garnish. Serve with raw quartered button
mushrooms, tomato wedges, broccoli florets and
carrot sticks.

Cottage Cheese and Caper Dip

MAKES ABOUT 450 ML/15 FL OZ

Capers have a Mediterranean flavour and
colourful pepper crudités complement this dip
well, adding a sunny appearance.

225 g/8 oz cottage cheese
3 Tbsp capers, chopped
150 ml/5 fl oz soured cream
1–2 Tbsp milk
1 spring onion, finely chopped
Freshly ground black pepper
Strips of red, green, yellow peppers and raddichio leaves

1. Place the cottage cheese in a small mixing
bowl, add the capers and soured cream, mixing
thoroughly. If the mixture is a little too thick, add
some of the milk.
2. Stir in the spring onion, reserving some for
garnish.
3. Season to taste with freshly ground black
pepper. Spoon the mixture into a serving dish,
sprinkle with the reserved chopped spring onion,
cover and refrigerate.
4. Serve with strips of colourful peppers and
raddichio leaves. This dip can also be served with
strips of deep-fried batter- or crumb-coated fish.

FISH
DIPS

2

Creamy Caviar Dip

MAKES ABOUT 375 ML/12 FL OZ

Creating a dip is one way of making a little caviar go a long way. If you cannot find real caviar, use lumpfish caviar instead.

150 g/5 oz double cream
1 Tbsp shallot, very finely chopped
1 lemon, with rind very finely grated
100 g/3½ oz jar caviar or lumpfish caviar
Freshly grated black pepper
Melba toast

1. Lightly whip the cream to a soft dropping consistency. Stir in the shallot, lemon rind and all but two teaspoons of the caviar. Season to taste with freshly ground black pepper. Cover and chill.
2. Spoon the dip into a serving dish and garnish with the reserved caviar. Serve with melba toast.

Caper and Tartare Dip

MAKES ABOUT 375 ML/12 FL OZ

This dip is ideal to serve with warm strips of crumb- or batter-covered white fish such as cod, haddock, or hoki that have been baked or deep fried.

50 g/2 oz small gherkins, plus enough for garnish
1 Tbsp capers
250 g/9 oz mayonnaise
1 Tbsp lemon juice
1 tsp white wine vinegar
2 Tbsp fresh parsley, chopped
1 Tbsp fresh chives, chopped
Freshly ground black pepper
Bread-crumb or batter-coated fish strips or nuggets,
strips of peppers and crisp lettuce leaves

1. Finely chop the gherkins and capers, reserving slices of gherkins for garnish.
2. Combine all of the ingredients together in a bowl. Season to taste with freshly ground black pepper. Cover and chill.
3. Transfer the dip to a serving bowl and serve with warm deep-fried or oven-baked fish strips, strips of raw bell peppers and crisp lettuce leaves.

Quick Anchovy Dip

MAKES ABOUT 300 ML/10 FL OZ

This speedy dip is packed with flavour.

50 g/2 oz canned anchovies in olive oil, drained
200 g/7 oz cream cheese
1 medium onion, chopped
1 garlic clove, crushed (optional)
1 Tbsp lemon juice
Freshly ground black pepper
1 Tbsp fresh chives, chopped
Green and black pitted olives, quartered button
mushrooms, strips of pepper, and chunks of Ciabatta or
olive bread

1. Place the anchovies, cream cheese, onion, garlic and lemon juice in a blender or food processor and process for a few seconds until smooth.
2. Turn the mixture into a bowl and season to taste with freshly ground black pepper. Cover and chill.
3. Spoon the mixture into a serving dish and garnish with chopped chives. Serve with pitted green and black olives, quartered button mushrooms, strips of pepper and chunks of bread, preferably Italian Ciabatta or olive bread.

Smoked Mackerel and Horseradish Dip

MAKES ABOUT 375 ML/12 FL OZ

Smoked mackerel and horseradish – both strong flavours made for each other.

150 g/5 oz smoked mackerel fillets, skin and bones removed
150 g/5 oz natural yogurt
3 Tbsp creamed horseradish sauce
1 Tbsp lemon juice
Freshly ground black pepper
Sprigs of parsley and lemon slices
Triangles of toasted white and brown bread

1. Break the fish into chunks and place in a mixing bowl. Carefully remove any small bones you may find.
2. Using the back of a fork, mash the fish into a paste consistency. Stir in the yogurt, horseradish sauce and lemon juice. Season to taste with freshly ground black pepper. Cover and chill.
3. Spoon the dip into a serving bowl and garnish with sprigs of parsley and lemon slices. Serve with warm triangles of toasted white and brown bread.

Creamy Tuna Dip

MAKES ABOUT 375 ML/12 FL OZ

200 g/7 oz canned tuna, well drained
125 g/4 oz low-calorie mayonnaise
50 g/2 oz low-fat natural yogurt
½ small lemon, juice and rind, finely grated
2 anchovy fillets
Freshly ground black pepper
Sprig of fresh parsley
Strips of celery, cucumber, baby sweet corn and tomato wedges

1. Place tuna in a mixing bowl. Using a fork, flake the fish into fine even pieces.
2. Stir in the mayonnaise, yogurt, lemon juice and rind.
3. Chop the anchovy fillets into small pieces and mash with the back of a fork on a small plate. Add to the dip.
4. Season to taste with freshly ground black pepper. Place in a serving bowl, cover and chill.
5. Garnish the dip with fresh parsley. Serve with strips of celery and cucumber, cooked and cooled baby sweet corn and tomato wedges.

Smoked Salmon and Lemon Dip

MAKES ABOUT 300 ML/10 FL OZ

This is an excellent dip served as a first course.

50 g/2 oz smoked salmon
200 g/7 oz cream cheese
3 Tbsp milk
1 lemon
1 Tbsp fresh dill, finely chopped
Fresh ground black pepper
Sprigs of dill and lemon slices
Melba toast, strips of cucumber, celery and carrot

1. Finely chop the smoked salmon. Soften the cream cheese in a bowl with the milk.
2. Finely grate the rind of the lemon. Add the rind and juice of the lemon to the softened cheese and mix together with the chopped salmon and dill. Season to taste with freshly ground black pepper. Cover and chill.
3. Spoon the dip into a serving bowl and garnish with sprigs of dill and lemon slices. Serve with melba toast, cucumber, celery and carrot.

Thai Coconut and Chilli Crab Dip

MAKES ABOUT 300 ML/10 FL OZ

Thai food has a wonderful fresh appearance and flavour – tempt your tastebuds with this dip.

175 ml/6 fl oz double cream
25 g/1 oz dessicated coconut
170 g/6 oz canned white crab meat, well drained
2 spring onions, finely chopped
1 Tbsp fresh coriander, finely chopped
2 Tbsp lime juice
1 red chilli, deseeded and finely chopped
Freshly ground black pepper
Fresh coriander leaves
Rice and prawn crackers, trimmed spring onions, strips of red pepper, cucumber and carrot

1. Place the cream and coconut in a small saucepan. Slowly bring the cream almost to the boil, then remove from the heat, stir and leave to infuse for ten minutes.

2. Strain the cream through a fine sieve into a bowl, pressing the coconut with a back of a spoon. Discard the coconut collected in the sieve. Leave the cream to cool completely.

3. Place the crab meat in a bowl and break apart into small pieces with a fork. Stir in the cooled cream, spring onions, chopped coriander, lime juice and chilli. Season well with freshly ground black pepper. Cover and chill.

4. Transfer the dip into a serving dish and garnish with coriander leaves. Serve with rice and prawn crackers, trimmed spring onions, and strips of red pepper, cucumber and carrot.

Devilled Egg and Tuna Dip

MAKES ABOUT 300 ML/10 FL OZ

Make this dip as fiery as you wish by adding as much chilli sauce as you can handle.

2 hard-boiled eggs
100 g/3½ oz canned tuna in water or oil, drained
150 g/5 oz mayonnaise
2 spring onions, finely chopped
A few drops of chilli sauce
Freshly ground black pepper
Tortilla crisps, toasted garlic bread and strips of celery

1. Remove the egg shells and chop the eggs very finely.
2. Mash the tuna with the back of a fork in a bowl. Add the egg, mayonnaise and all but one tablespoon of the chopped spring onion. Mix thoroughly.
3. Add sufficient chilli sauce to taste and season well with freshly ground black pepper. Cover and chill.
4. Turn the dip into a serving dish and garnish with the reserved chopped spring onion. Serve with spicy tortilla crisps, toasted garlic bread, and strips of celery.

Chive and Smoked Oyster Dip

MAKES ABOUT 300 ML/10 FL OZ

2 105 g/3½ oz cans smoked oysters in oil, well drained (you require about 175 g/6 oz drained weight of oysters)
2 Tbsp fresh chives, chopped
150 ml/5 fl oz soured cream
Freshly ground black pepper
Melba toast

1. Reserve two oysters and a few chopped chives for garnish.
2. Place the remaining oysters and soured cream into a blender or food processor and process for a few seconds until smooth. Turn into a bowl and stir in the chives. Season well with freshly ground black pepper. Cover and chill.
3. Transfer the dip to a serving dish and garnish with the reserved oysters. Sprinkle with the chives. Serve with melba toast.

Avocado and Tuna Dip

MAKES ABOUT 375 ML/12 FL OZ

1 medium ripe avocado
2 Tbsp lemon juice
100 g/3½ oz canned tuna, well drained
125 g/4 oz mayonnaise
2 to 3 drops Worcester sauce
½ tsp English mustard
Freshly ground black pepper
Sprigs of flat-leaf parsley and strips of lemon rind
Cheese straws, strips of courgettes, carrot, green beans

1. Using a sharp knife, halve the avocado lengthwise. Carefully twist the two halves in opposing directions to separate the avocado. Remove the stone and skin.
2. Cut the avocado flesh into chunks and place in a bowl with the lemon juice. Using a fork, mash the avocado into a pulp.
3. Flake the tuna into the avocado mixture. Add the mayonnaise, Worcester sauce and mustard, mixing thoroughly. Season to taste with freshly ground black pepper. Cover and chill.
4. Transfer the dip to a serving bowl, garnish with sprigs of parsley and lemon rind. Serve with cheese straws, strips of courgettes and carrot, and blanched and cooled green beans.

Taramasalata

MAKES ABOUT 375 ML/12 FL OZ

If possible use fresh smoked cod roe (fish eggs) or smoked soft roe – for this you may have to find a speciality fishmonger. If fresh cod roe is hard to find, then use "tamara" (pale orange carp roe) or red (whitefish) caviar.

200 g/7 oz fresh smoked cod roe
1 slice of white bread, crust removed
1 garlic clove, crushed
175 ml/6 fl oz olive oil
Juice of ½ lemon
Freshly ground black pepper
Sprig of fresh parsley and lemon slices
Strips of warm pitta bread

1. Place the roe in a bowl. Hold the bread under cold running water to wet it. Squeeze the excess water from the bread, then add it to the roe, along with the garlic. Mix thoroughly.
2. Add the olive oil *very gradually*, to the roe mixture, beating in each small addition thoroughly. It is important not to rush this stage or else the mixture will separate and curdle. The mixture should be smooth, pink and creamy looking.
3. Stir in the lemon juice and season well with freshly ground black pepper. Cover and chill.
4. Spoon the taramasalata into a serving dish, garnish with the parsley and lemon slices. Serve with strips of warm pitta bread.

Bagna Cauda

MAKES ABOUT 300 ML/10 FL OZ

If possible, keep this dip warm in a heatproof dish on a tabletop warmer or over a nightlight, while you and your friends dip into it with a selection of raw vegetables and bread.

50 g/2 oz canned anchovy fillets, drained
3 garlic cloves
4 Tbsp olive oil
4 Tbsp butter
150 g/5 oz double cream
Freshly ground black pepper
Strips of fennel, celery and carrot and cubed, crusty bread

1. Finely chop the anchovy fillets and crush the cloves of garlic.
2. Heat the olive oil and butter together and gently sauté the garlic for one minute. Add the anchovies and simmer over a low heat for ten minutes.
3. Remove from the heat and allow to cool slightly before pouring in the cream, mixing thoroughly. Return the pan to the heat and heat through gently. Season well with freshly ground black pepper. Serve the dip warm with strips of fennel, celery, carrot and cubes of crusty bread.

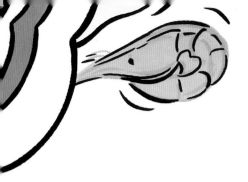

Prawn Cocktail Dip

MAKES ABOUT 300 ML/10 FL OZ

Use a selection of small crisp lettuce leaves to scoop up this dip.

175 g/6 oz cooked shelled prawns (thawed, if frozen)
150 g/5 oz mayonnaise
1 tsp tomato paste
1 tsp white wine vinegar
3 to 5 drops chilli sauce
1 small lemon
Freshly ground black pepper
Small crisp lettuce leaves, celery, cucumber strips and melba toast

1. Drain any excess liquid from the prawns. Chop them finely.
2. In a bowl, combine the mayonnaise, tomato purée, vinegar and as many drops of chilli sauce to suit your own taste. I usually find three to five drops give a nice piquancy without being overpowering.
3. Cut the lemon in half, reserving one half for garnish. Finely grate the rind, squeeze the juice from the other lemon half, and stir into the dip.
4. Mix the chopped prawns into the mayonnaise mixture and season to taste with freshly ground black pepper. Cover and chill.
5. Spoon the dip into a serving dish and garnish with slices of lemon. Serve with a selection of individual crisp lettuce leaves, celery, cucumber strips and melba toast.

Crab Dip

MAKES ABOUT 375 ML/12 FL OZ

If you prefer a smoother-textured crab dip, you can purée everything together in a blender or food processor, but I feel it then loses its crab-meat texture. To add to the seaside feel of this dip, serve it in several large cleaned crab shells, if you can find them.

175 g/6 oz canned white crab meat, drained
150 g/5 oz fromage frais
1 Tbsp lemon juice
1 tsp white wine vinegar
2 Tbsp fresh parsley, chopped
Freshly ground black pepper
Sprigs of fresh parsley
Crisps and salty snacks

1. Place the crab meat in a bowl and with the back of a fork mash it into a fine shredded consistency.
2. Stir in the fromage frais, lemon juice, wine vinegar, and parsley. Season well with freshly ground black pepper to taste. Cover and chill.
3. Spoon the dip into a serving bowl and garnish with sprigs of parsley. Serve with a selection of crisps and other salty snacks.

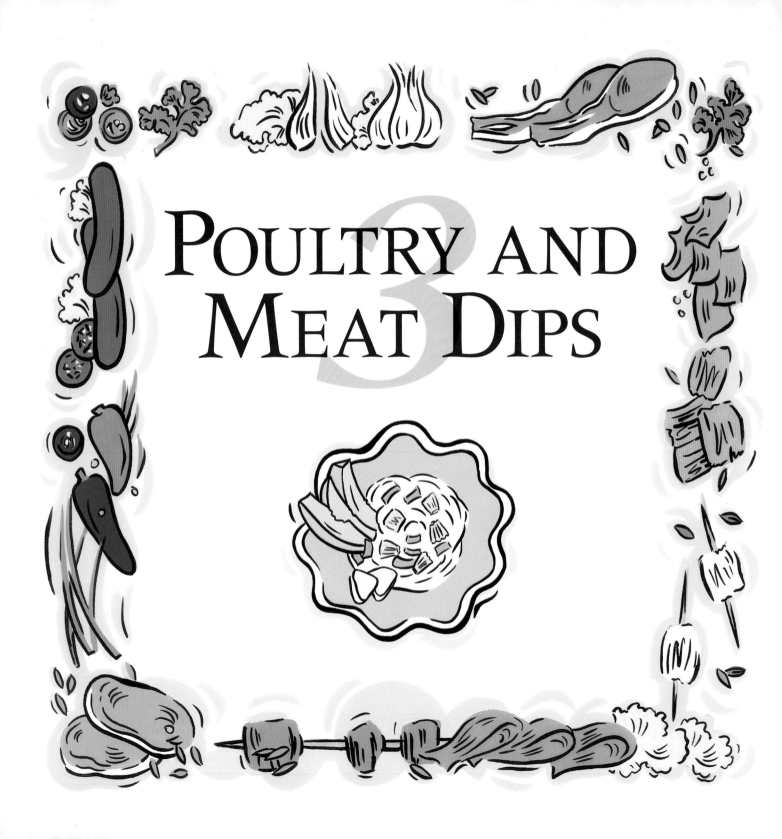

POULTRY AND MEAT DIPS 3

Peanut Satay Style Dip with Stir-Fried Pork Strips

MAKES ABOUT 300 ML/10 FL OZ

This Thai-based recipe has a rich peanut dip and is excellent served with marinated stir-fried strips of lean pork. Use fillet (tenderloin) of pork because it is a tender cut that can easily be stirfried. Serve both the dip and meat hot, straight from the pan. This will serve about six to eight people as a first course or four people as a main meal.

FOR THE DIP
25 g/1 oz dessicated coconut
250 ml/8 fl oz milk
1 tsp sunflower oil
2 cm/1 in piece of fresh ginger root, peeled and finely chopped
1 garlic clove, crushed
1 green chilli, deseeded and finely chopped
175 g/6 oz crunchy peanut butter

FOR THE STIR-FRIED PORK STRIPS
450 g/1 lb fillet (tenderloin) of pork
3 Tbsp medium dry sherry
2 Tbsp dark soy sauce
2 tsp red wine vinegar
3 Tbsp sunflower oil, for frying

1. Cut the pork into thin bite-sized strips. Combine the sherry, soy sauce and vinegar in a large bowl and add the pork, stirring well to ensure it is well coated in the marinade. Cover and chill until required for cooking.
2. Meanwhile, place the coconut and milk in a small, heavy-based saucepan and slowly bring to the boil, taking care not to scorch the milk. Remove from the heat and leave the coconut to infuse in the milk for at least thirty minutes.
3. To make the Dip: Strain the infused coconut and milk through a fine sieve over a bowl. Gently press the coconut with the back of a spoon to express as much coconut-flavoured milk as possible. Discard the coconut.
4. Heat the sunflower oil in a saucepan and gently sauté the ginger, garlic and chilli for two to three minutes until tender, but not browned. Add the coconut-flavoured milk and peanut butter. Heat gently, stirring continuously until the peanut butter has melted and combined with the other ingredients to make a smooth sauce. Simmer gently for five minutes. Remove from heat but keep warm until serving.
5. To stir-fry the Pork Strips: Heat the sunflower oil in a large frying pan or wok and cook the pork in several batches, stir-frying for about five to eight minutes, or until the meat is thoroughly cooked. The meat will turn a delicious brown colour and the juices should be clear rather than bloody. Remove the cooked pork to a serving dish and keep warm while cooking the remaining batches.
6. Spoon the peanut dip into a heatproof serving dish and serve with the stir-fried pork strips. If serving this as a main meal you may wish to serve vegetable accompaniments such as strips of cucumber and peppers and trimmed spring onions.

Quick Tangy Tomato Dip with Turkey Dipping Sticks

MAKES ABOUT 250 ML/8 FL OZ

SERVES SIX AS A STARTER, FOUR AS A MAIN MEAL WITH ACCOMPANIMENTS

Bread-crumb and batter-coated nuggets or strips of meats and fish are readily available from most supermarkets, fresh or frozen, but sometimes it's great to have a go yourself and make your own. This quick and easy batter recipe can be applied to many of the other dips since the batter can coat fish, meat, poultry and vegetables such as onion rings or courgette slices. It is also used to coat apple rings (see the sweet Cinnamon and Raisin Yogurt Dip on page 57). Happy dipping!

FOR THE DIP
4 Tbsp ketchup
4 Tbsp pourable honey
1 Tbsp light brown sugar
1 Tbsp red wine vinegar
50 ml/2 fl oz fresh orange juice
2–3 drops of chilli sauce
1 tsp dry sherry

FOR THE TURKEY DIPPING STICKS
BATTER
MAKES ABOUT 300 ML/10 FL OZ

125 g/4 oz plain flour
Salt and pepper
1 egg, beaten
175 ml/6 fl oz milk

TURKEY STICKS
450 g/1lb skinless and boneless turkey breast meat
50 g/2 oz flour, seasoned with salt and pepper
Vegetable oil, for deep frying

To accompany if serving as a main meal: French fries, raw strips of celery, cucumber and courgettes

1. To make the Dip: Simply combine all the dip ingredients together in a bowl. Cover and chill.

2. To make the Batter: Sift the flour into a bowl and season with salt and pepper, making a well in the centre. Combine the beaten egg with the milk and gradually blend into the flour, using a fork to make a smooth batter. This can be made well in advance, covered and kept in the refrigerator until required.

3. To make the Turkey Sticks: Cut the turkey breast meat into even-sized pieces about 5 cm by 5 mm (2 in by ¼ in). Place the seasoned flour in a small, clean plastic bag and add about a quarter of the turkey strips at a time. Hold the bag at the top to seal and shake the turkey strips until evenly coated in the flour. Remove the coated turkey from the bag to a plate and repeat for the remaining turkey.

4. Heat the oil in a large heavy-based pan to 180°C/355°F. Dip the coated turkey strips a few at a time in the batter, allowing the excess batter to run from the meat. Fry in the oil for about eight to ten minutes, until golden and the turkey is thoroughly cooked through. Drain on paper towels and keep warm while frying the remaining batter-coated turkey in batches.

5. Serve the warm turkey strips with the dip, which can be served chilled or warm. If serving as a main meal, accompany the dip with French fries and strips of celery, cucumber and courgettes.

Ham and Gruyere Dip

MAKES ABOUT 375 ML/12 FL OZ

Gruyère cheese has a sweet flavour and delicious nutty aroma that complements the ham in this dip. Served in hollowed-out crusty bread rolls with strips of raw cucumber, celery and carrot, this makes a filling lunchtime snack.

200 g/7 oz soured cream
½ tsp Dijon mustard
75 g/3 oz cooked lean ham
75 g/3 oz Gruyère cheese
1 Tbsp fresh parsley, chopped
Freshly ground black pepper
Hollowed-out crusty bread rolls (optional)
Strips of cucumber, celery and carrot

1. Place the soured cream and mustard in a bowl and mix thoroughly.

2. Finely dice the ham. Finely grate the Gruyère cheese. Add the ham and cheese to the soured cream and combine well. Stir in the parsley. Season well with freshly ground black pepper.

3. Transfer the dip to a serving bowl or hollowed-out crusty bread rolls. Serve with strips of cucumber, celery and carrot.

Smoky Bacon and Cream Cheese Dip

MAKES ABOUT 300 ML/10 FL OZ

For best effect chill this dip for at least two hours so that the smoky bacon flavour matures in the cream cheese.

175 g/6 oz smoked bacon rashers, cooked until crispy
200 g/7 oz cream cheese
75 ml/3 oz natural yogurt
2 Tbsp milk
Freshly ground black pepper
1 Tbsp fresh chives, chopped
Breadsticks, a selection of crackers and strips of celery

1. Blend the cream cheese, yogurt and milk together in a bowl.

2. Crumble the cooked bacon into little pieces. Reserve one tablespoon for garnish and stir the remaining bacon into the cream cheese mixture. Season well with freshly ground black pepper. Cover and chill.

3. Spoon the dip into a serving dish and sprinkle with the chopped chives and reserved crumbled bacon. Serve with breadsticks, a selection of crackers and strips of celery.

Smoked Ham and Pineapple Dip

MAKES ABOUT 375 ML/12 FL OZ

This dip needs to be chilled to allow the smoked ham flavour to mingle with the cream cheese. Serve the dip with bite-sized wedges of peeled mango, paw-paw, and melon for a tropical flourish.

200 g/7 oz cream cheese
125 g/4 oz cooked smoked ham, sliced
225 g/8 oz canned pineapple pieces in natural juice, drained
Freshly ground black pepper
Sprig of fresh parsley
Small wedges of peeled mango, paw-paw and melon

1. Place the cream cheese, half of the smoked ham and half of the pineapple pieces into a blender or food processor and process for a few seconds until smooth. Transfer the mixture to a bowl.
2. Finely chop the remaining ham and pineapple pieces and lightly stir into the cheese mixture to add colour and texture. Season well with freshly ground black pepper. Cover and chill.
3. Spoon the dip into a serving dish and garnish with a sprig of fresh parsley. Serve with peeled, bite-sized wedges of mango, paw-paw and melon.

Beef and Creamed Horseradish Dip

MAKES ABOUT 375 ML/12 FL OZ

This dip makes an excellent casual lunch and is great to eat with fresh French fries while watching television.

200 g/7 oz soured cream
125 g/4 oz cooked lean beef, chopped
2 tsp creamed horseradish sauce
Freshly ground black pepper
Sprigs of fresh parsley
Wedges of tomato, crisp lettuce leaves and French fries

1. Place the soured cream, cooked beef and horseradish sauce in a blender or food processor and process for a few seconds until smooth. Transfer to a bowl and season well with freshly ground black pepper. Cover and chill.
2. Spoon the dip into a serving dish or individual ramekins and garnish with sprigs of fresh parsley. Serve with wedges of tomato, crisp lettuce leaves and plenty of hot French fries for a hearty feast.

Roasted Peanut and Ham Dip

MAKES ABOUT 375 ML/12 FL OZ

150 g/5 oz soured cream
125 g/4 oz smoked lean ham slices, chopped
125 g/4 oz roasted peanuts, coarsely chopped
5 to 6 drops Worcester sauce
Pinch of cayenne pepper
Breadsticks, crisps, crackers, a selection of raw strips of vegetables such as celery, cucumber, carrot and wedges of tomato

1. Place the soured cream and ham in a blender or food processor and process for a few seconds until smooth and well combined. Turn the ham mixture into a bowl.
2. Add the peanuts, reserving a tablespoonful for garnish.
3. Season the dip with Worcester sauce and cayenne pepper. Cover and chill.
4. Transfer the dip to a serving bowl and garnish with the reserved peanuts. Serve with breadsticks, crisps and crackers, plus raw strips of celery, cucumber, and carrot and wedges of tomato.

Chorizo Sausage and Tomato Dip

MAKES ABOUT 375 ML/12 FL OZ

Chorizo sausages are Spanish cooked sausages with a spicy, garlic flavour. If you cannot find Chorizo sausages, use any cooked garlic sausage. Serve with chunks of crusty bread or garlic bread to scoop out the spicy sausage.

1 Tbsp olive oil
2 Tbsp onion, finely chopped
150 g/5 oz Chorizo sausages, finely chopped
395 g/14 oz canned chopped tomatoes, drained
1 tsp tomato paste
1 tsp fresh thyme leaves, stalks removed
Chunks of crusty bread or garlic bread

1. Heat the oil in a saucepan and add the onion and Chorizo sausages. Sauté for five minutes over moderate heat, until the onion is tender.
2. Add the tomatoes, tomato paste and thyme and simmer for ten minutes. Turn into a heatproof serving dish and serve warm with crusty bread or garlic bread.

Chicken Liver and Mushroom Dip

MAKES ABOUT 375 ML/12 FL OZ

This has the richness of a pâté but the moister texture of a dip. It will serve six to eight as a starter, four to six as a snack lunch.

4 Tbsp olive oil
1 medium onion, chopped
1 garlic clove, crushed
200 g/7 oz open mushrooms, finely chopped
227 g/8 oz chicken livers, cut into even-sized pieces
1 Tbsp brandy (optional)
Salt and freshly ground black pepper
2 Tbsp fresh parsley, chopped
Melba toast, ryebread and crackers

1. Heat the olive oil in a saucepan. Sauté the onion and garlic for about four to five minutes over moderate heat, until tender, but not browned. Stir occasionally.
2. Add the mushrooms to the onion mixture. Cook over moderate heat for about five minutes until the mushrooms have cooked down.
3. Add the chicken livers to the pan. Simmer for about five minutes, stirring occasionally, until the chicken livers are cooked. Test by cutting a piece in half: the liver should be grey in colour with no blood present. As soon as the liver is cooked, remove from the heat, transfer to a bowl, and allow to cool for ten minutes.
4. Place the cooled chicken liver mixture into a blender or food processor, along with the brandy, if desired. Process until smooth. Season to taste with salt and black pepper. Cover and chill.
5. Spoon the dip into a serving dish and sprinkle with the chopped parsley. Serve with melba toast, ryebread and crackers.

Chicken and Almond Dip

MAKES ABOUT 450 ML/15 FL OZ

The celery and toasted almonds add a surprising crunch to this creamy chicken dip.

50 g/2 oz chopped blanched almonds
150 g/5 oz cooked boneless and skinless chicken breast
200 g/7 oz full-fat natural yogurt
2 celery sticks, finely chopped
Freshly ground black pepper
Cubed bagels or crusty bread, strips of cucumber, carrot,
peppers and courgettes

1. Sprinkle the chopped almonds in a single layer on a sheet of aluminium foil. Place under a hot pre-heated grill and toast until a pale golden brown, turning occasionally, so they brown evenly. Take care that they don't brown too suddenly. Remove from the grill and allow to cool completely.
2. Coarsely chop the chicken and place in a blender or food processor along with the yogurt. Process for a few seconds until smooth. Turn the chicken mixture into a bowl.
3. Reserve a tablespoon of chopped celery and toasted almonds for a garnish and mix the remaining celery and nuts into the chicken mixture. Season well with freshly ground black pepper. Cover and chill.
4. To serve, spoon the dip into a serving bowl and sprinkle with the reserved chopped celery and toasted almonds. Serve with cubed pieces of bagel or crusty bread and strips of cucumber, carrot, peppers and courgettes.

VEGETABLE DIPS

Tzatziki

MAKES ABOUT 300 ML/10 FL OZ

With this traditional, chilled Greek dip, cut small firm courgettes into long thin strips, coat in seasoned flour, and pan-fry in olive oil until golden – serve warm.

½ cucumber (18 cm/7 in)
150 ml/5 fl oz full fat yogurt
1 garlic clove, crushed
1 tsp white wine vinegar
3 Tbsp fresh mint, chopped
1 Tbsp olive oil
Freshly ground black pepper
Cucumber slices and mint sprigs
Pan-fried strips of courgettes

1. Peel the cucumber, cut in half lengthwise. Using a teaspoon, scoop out the seeds. Coarsely grate the cucumber flesh into a bowl. Drain any excess liquid collected in the bowl from the grated cucumber.
2. Add the yogurt, garlic, vinegar, mint and olive oil to the cucumber and mix well. Season well with freshly ground black pepper. Cover and chill.
3. Transfer the tzatziki to a serving dish and garnish with cucumber slices and sprigs of mint. Serve with warm, pan-fried courgettes strips.

Watercress and Yogurt Dip

MAKES ABOUT 300 ML/10 FL OZ

125 g/4 oz fresh watercress, washed
150 g/5 oz natural low-fat yogurt
Freshly ground black pepper
Crisp small lettuce leaves, celery and carrot strips; cooked salmon or white fish pieces, crumb- or batter-coated

1. Reserve a few watercress sprigs for a garnish. Make sure the watercress is well drained, then place in a blender or food processor with the yogurt and process for a few seconds until well combined. Season with freshly ground black pepper.
2. Pour the dip into a serving dish and garnish with the watercress sprigs. Serve with small, crisp lettuce leaves with which to scoop up the dip and strips of celery and carrot. Salmon strips coated in bread crumbs or batter, and fried or baked, are wonderful served warm with this dip, although any white fish such as cod, hoki or haddock served in this way are all extremely good accompaniments.

Black Olive Dip

MAKES ABOUT 375 ML/12 FL OZ

400 g/14 oz canned pitted black olives, drained
2 garlic cloves, crushed
1 Tbsp tomato paste
1 Tbsp olive oil
1 beefsteak tomato, skinned, deseeded, and finely chopped
Freshly ground black pepper
Fresh basil leaves
Thin wedges of olive bread or Ciabatta

1. Place the drained olives, garlic, tomato paste and olive oil in a blender or food processor and process for a few seconds so that the olives retain some texture and are not completely smooth.
2. Transfer the mixture to a bowl and stir in the chopped tomato. Season well with freshly ground black pepper. Cover and chill.
3. Transfer the dip to a serving bowl and garnish with fresh basil leaves. Serve with wedges of olive bread or Ciabatta.

Scarlet Delight Dip

MAKES ABOUT 375 ML/12 FL OZ

This dip has a stunning appearance but is not for the faint-hearted. It tastes wonderful on any occasion but its beet-red colour makes it particularly well suited for a Halloween party!

1 orange
200 g/7 oz cooked beetroot
150 g/5 oz soured cream
Freshly ground black pepper
Strips of fennel, celery, courgettes and cucumber

1. Make the orange rind garnish: With a zester or vegetable peeler, remove a few strips of rind from the orange. If using a vegetable peeler, the pieces of rind will need to be cut into very fine strips with a sharp knife.

2. Roughly chop the cooked beetroot and place in a blender or food processor with the juice from the orange and blend until smooth.

3. Tip the beetroot mixture into a bowl and add three-quarters of the soured cream, mixing thoroughly. Season to taste with freshly ground black pepper. Cover and chill.

4. To serve, turn the beetroot dip into a serving dish and lightly swirl in the remaining soured cream. Garnish with the orange rind. Serve with strips of fennel, celery, courgettes and cucumber.

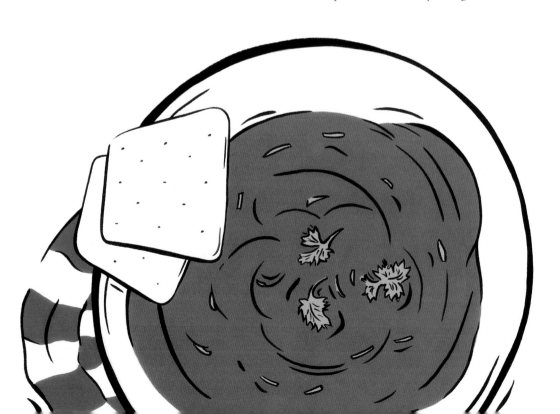

Spring Onion Dip

MAKES ABOUT 300 ML/10 FL OZ

75 g/3 oz spring onions, finely chopped
150 g/5 oz soured cream
75 g/3 oz natural yogurt
1 tsp paprika
Freshly ground black pepper
Crisp lettuce leaves, strips of courgettes and peppers,
and potato crisps

1. Reserve one tablespoon of the chopped spring onions for garnish. Place the remaining spring onions, soured cream, yogurt and paprika in a bowl and mix thoroughly. Season to taste with freshly ground black pepper. Cover and chill.
2. Spoon the dip into a serving bowl and sprinkle with the reserved chopped spring onions. Serve with crisp lettuce leaves, strips of courgettes and peppers and potato crisps.

Sweet and Sour Dip with Chinese Vegetables

MAKES ABOUT 450 ML/15 FL OZ

1 Tbsp peanut oil
2 spring onions, chopped
1 small yellow pepper, deseeded and finely chopped
1 small green pepper, deseeded and finely chopped
395 g/14 oz canned chopped tomatoes, drained
2 Tbsp red wine vinegar
1 Tbsp dry sherry
1 Tbsp light brown sugar
Strips of celery, cucumber, carrot, yellow and red peppers,
canned water chestnuts (drained), baby sweet corn and
mange tout (blanched and chilled), and prawn crackers

1. Heat the oil in a saucepan and fry the spring onions and peppers for about five minutes over a moderate heat until tender but not browned, stirring occasionally.
2. Add the tomatoes, vinegar, sherry and brown sugar. Simmer for five minutes, remove from the heat, and allow to cool. Cover and chill.
3. Transfer the dip to a serving bowl and serve with strips of raw vegetables, drained canned water chestnuts, and briefly blanched baby sweetcorn and mange tout. Prawn crackers are also ideal dipping accompaniments.

Radish Dip

MAKES ABOUT 375 ML/12 FL OZ

This pretty pink dip has a refreshingly light flavour.

150 g/5 oz radishes, leaves removed
125 g/4 oz mayonnaise
150 g/5 oz soured cream
2 tsp lemon juice
Freshly ground black pepper
Crisp lettuce leaves, strips of cucumber and celery, cooked
peeled jumbo prawns

1. Reserve one radish for garnish. Place the remaining radishes in a food processor with a fine grater disc or finely grate the radishes by hand. Drain any excess liquid.
2. Turn the grated radish into a bowl and stir in the mayonnaise, soured cream, and lemon juice. Season well with freshly ground black pepper. Cover and chill.
3. Turn the dip into a serving bowl and garnish with slices cut from the reserved radish. Serve with crisp lettuce leaves, strips of cucumber and celery, and cooked, peeled jumbo prawns.

Tomato and Basil Dip

MAKES ABOUT 375 ML/12 FL OZ

This dip makes a colourful first course. It can be prepared in advance and served in hollowed-out tomatoes.

4 beefsteak tomatoes
1 small onion, chopped
6 Tbsp fresh basil, chopped
Freshly ground black pepper
Fresh basil leaves
Breadsticks, strips of cucumber, celery and courgettes

1. To hollow out the tomatoes, first cut the top off the tomatoes in a thin slice. With a sharp knife, cut around the inner flesh of each of the tomatoes and scoop out the central flesh and seeds with a spoon. Place the four hollowed-out tomatoes upside down on a plate to allow excess juice to drain out.
2. Discard the tomato seeds and finely dice the tomato flesh. Place the chopped tomato in a non-metallic sieve and press out any excess juice.
3. Place half the chopped tomato and all of the chopped onion in a blender or food processor and process for a few seconds until smooth. Transfer the mixture to a bowl.
4. Stir in the remaining chopped tomato and chopped fresh basil. Season well with freshly ground black pepper. Divide the dip mixture evenly among the four hollowed-out tomatoes. Cover and chill.
5. Garnish with fresh basil leaves just before serving. Serve with breadsticks and strips of cucumber, celery and courgettes.

Sun-dried Tomato Stunner Dip

MAKES ABOUT 375 ML/12 FL OZ

Sun-dried tomatoes give this dip a really rich flavour, so serve it with strips of peppers and slices of warm garlic bread.

395 g/14 oz canned tomatoes in tomato juice, drained and chopped
1 small yellow pepper
75 g/3 oz sun-dried tomatoes in oil, drained
1 Tbsp fresh basil, chopped
1 Tbsp fresh oregano, chopped
Freshly ground black pepper
Fresh basil and oregano leaves
Strips of yellow, orange, red, and green pepper, warm garlic bread, sliced

1. Cut the yellow pepper in half lengthwise and remove the stalk and seeds. Roughly chop one-half of the pepper and place in a blender or food processor along with the tomatoes and sun-dried tomatoes. Process for a few seconds until smooth.
2. Transfer the tomato mixture to a bowl and stir in the chopped basil and oregano. Finely dice the remaining half of the yellow pepper and add to the dip. Season with freshly ground black pepper. Cover and chill.
3. Spoon the dip into a serving dish and garnish with basil and oregano leaves. Serve with strips of colourful peppers and slices of warm garlic bread.

Puréed Vegetable and Pumpkin Seed Dip

MAKES ABOUT 375 ML/12 FL OZ

This dip can be served hot or cold.

1 Tbsp olive oil
1 medium onion, finely chopped
1 garlic clove, crushed (optional)
1 small yellow-fleshed squash (you need about 200 g/7 oz chopped flesh)
1 medium red pepper
1 tsp fresh thyme leaves
50 ml/2 fl oz vegetable stock OR cold water
3 Tbsp pumpkin seeds
Small wedges of a selection of breads, e.g. Ciabatta, tomato bread, olive bread and pumpernickel

1. Heat the olive oil in a saucepan, add the onion and garlic, and sauté gently for five minutes, until tender but not browned. Stir occasionally.

2. Meanwhile, cut the squash in half and scoop out the seeds. Cut the halves into wedges and using a sharp knife, remove the squash skin. Cut the squash flesh into 2 cm (1 in) pieces. Cut the red pepper in half lengthwise, remove the seeds and dice the pepper flesh.

3. Add the squash, red pepper, and thyme to the onion and fry for two minutes. Add the vegetable stock OR cold water, bring to the boil, cover and simmer for fifteen minutes, or until the squash is just tender. Stir occasionally. Allow to cool for at least ten minutes before puréeing.

4. Lightly toast the pumpkin seeds under a hot preheated grill – this only takes a minute or two, so don't leave them unattended! The pumpkin seeds begin to make a popping sound when they are ready. Remove from the grill and leave to cool.

5. Place the vegetable mixture and all but one tablespoon of the pumpkin seeds into a blender or food processor. Process for a few seconds on a pulse setting if possible, so that the dip retains some texture rather than being completely smooth.

6. Transfer to a serving dish and serve warm or allow to cool, then cover and chill in the refrigerator. Sprinkle with the remaining toasted pumpkin seeds just before serving. Serve with a selection of flavoured breads such as Ciabatta, tomato, olive and pumpernickel cut into suitable dipping-sized wedges.

Quick and Easy BBQ Dip

MAKES ABOUT 375 ML/12 FL OZ

Serve this dip warm or cold and don't just wait for the barbecue season – it tastes as good with grilled chicken drumsticks, spare ribs and sausages as it does with grilled yellow and green pepper quarters.

1 Tbsp olive oil
1 medium onion, finely chopped
395 g/14 oz canned tomatoes in juice, chopped
2 Tbsp brown sauce
2 tsp soft brown sugar
Chilli sauce
Barbecued or well grilled chicken drumsticks, spare ribs, sausages and yellow and green pepper

1. Heat the olive oil in a saucepan and fry the chopped onion for about five minutes, until tender and lightly browned.
2. Meanwhile, drain the chopped tomatoes, reserving the juice.
3. Add the drained tomatoes, brown sauce and sugar to the frying onions. Add a few drops of chilli sauce to taste. Simmer the dip for ten minutes, adding a little of the reserved tomato juice if the dip becomes too thick.
4. Serve the dip warm or cool – cover and chill in the refrigerator until required. Serve with barbecued or well grilled chicken drumsticks, spare ribs, sausages and quarters of yellow and green peppers that have been grilled until slightly charred.

Guacamole

MAKES ABOUT 450 ML/15 FL OZ

2 medium ripe avocados
3 Tbsp lemon juice
1 garlic clove, crushed
2 tomatoes, chopped, skinned and deseeded
2 spring onions, finely chopped
1 green chilli, deseeded and finely chopped
1 Tbsp fresh coriander, finely chopped
Freshly ground black pepper
Tortilla crisps and strips of pepper

1. Cut the avocados in half lengthwise. Twist the halves in opposite directions to separate the two halves. Remove the central stone and peel away the skin. Chop the avocado flesh into chunks.
2. Place the avocado in a mixing bowl along with the lemon juice and garlic and mash with the back of a fork until fairly smooth.
3. In a small bowl, mix together the tomato, spring onions, chilli and coriander. Reserve one tablespoon of the mix for garnish and add the rest to the avocado mixture. Combine thoroughly. Season to taste with freshly ground black pepper.
4. Place the guacamole in a serving dish and garnish with the reserved tomato, spring onions, chilli and coriander. Cover and chill.
5. Serve the guacamole dip with tortilla crisps and colourful strips of pepper. For those who like it hot, raw chillies can also be dipped!

Aubergine and Pepper Dip

MAKES ABOUT 375 ML/12 FL OZ

Grilled vegetables add a delicious Mediterranean flavour to this dip. The aubergine does not necessarily have to be peeled.

1 aubergine (weighing about 350 g/12 oz)
1 medium onion
1 medium green pepper
1 garlic clove (optional)
50 ml/2 fl oz olive oil
Freshly ground black pepper
Slices of warm garlic bread

1. Preheat the grill. Cut the aubergine into 1 cm (1 in) rounds, discarding the top stalk. Peel the onion and also cut into slices. Halve the green pepper lengthways.

2. Place the aubergine, onion, pepper halves (skin side facing up) and garlic clove onto a heatproof tray, brush with olive oil and season with freshly ground black pepper. Place the vegetables under the grill and cook for about fifteen minutes, until the aubergine slices turn a golden brown and the onion rings caramelize. When one side is browned, turn them over, brush with olive oil, season and cook until browned. The green pepper should be cooked until the skin blackens and the garlic clove should soften and the skin char.

3. When the vegetables are cooked, remove them to a dish and allow to cool completely.

4. Remove the blackened skin from the cooled green pepper. Remove the stalk and seeds and chop the cooked pepper flesh.

5. Place all of the cooked vegetables in a blender or food processor and process for a few seconds until smooth. Spoon into a bowl, cover and chill.

6. Serve with slices of warm crusty garlic bread.

Smooth Chilli Tomato Dip

MAKES ABOUT 450 ML/15 FL OZ

This cheerful and fiery red dip can be served warm or chilled. If served warm with plenty of dipping accompaniments, it makes a substantial main meal.

2 Tbsp olive oil
1 medium onion, finely chopped
3 red chillies, deseeded and finely chopped
2 garlic cloves, crushed
400 g/14 oz canned plum tomatoes
1 tsp red wine vinegar
2 tsp caster sugar
Freshly ground black pepper
Cooked, peeled jumbo prawns, deep-fried batter-coated vegetables, e.g. onion rings, cauliflower and broccoli florets; strips of pitta bread and peppers

1. Heat the olive oil in a saucepan, add the onion, chillies and garlic. Sauté gently for five minutes, stirring occasionally.

2. Add the canned tomatoes and their juice, the vinegar and sugar to the fried onion mixture. Break the tomatoes up with a wooden spoon. Bring to the boil, cover and simmer for twenty-five minutes.

3. Allow to cool for ten minutes before processing in a blender or food processor until smooth. Season to taste with freshly ground black pepper. Turn into a heatproof serving dish if serving warm, or allow to cool completely then chill in the refrigerator, if serving cold. Serve with peeled, cooked jumbo prawns, deep-fried batter-coated vegetables and strips of pitta bread and colourful peppers.

Sesame and Red Pepper Dip

MAKES ABOUT 450 ML/15 FL OZ

A distinctive taste of the Orient adds a characteristic note to this sesame dip.

1 Tbsp sunflower oil
½ tsp sesame oil
2.5 cm (1 in) cube root ginger, peeled and finely chopped
1 garlic clove, crushed
400 g/14 oz red peppers, deseeded and finely diced
150 ml/5 fl oz chicken OR vegetable stock
2 Tbsp medium dry sherry
1 Tbsp sesame seeds
Rice and prawn crackers; blanched and cooled mange tout and baby sweet corn; strips of celery and cucumber

1. Heat the sunflower and sesame oil in a saucepan, add the ginger and garlic, and sauté gently for two to three minutes until softened but not browned. Add the peppers and sauté for another five minutes.
2. Add the stock and sherry, bring to the boil, and simmer for fifteen minutes. Leave to cool.
3. Meanwhile, place the sesame seeds in a single layer on a sheet of aluminium foil on a baking tray. Place under a moderately hot grill for about two to three minutes, until lightly browned. Turn them occasionally so they toast evenly and take care that they do not brown suddenly. Remove from the grill and leave to cool.
4. Place the cooled red pepper mixture into a blender or food processor, retaining some of the cooking liquid in the saucepan. Add half of the toasted sesame seeds and process for a few seconds until the mixture is smooth – don't worry if some of the sesame seeds remain unblended. Check the consistency of the red pepper mixture: If it is too firm for a dip, add a little of the reserved cooking liquid until you obtain a fairly thin consistency.
5. Transfer the dip to a serving dish and chill until required.
6. Just before serving, sprinkle with the remaining toasted sesame seeds. Serve with rice and prawn crackers, blanched and cooled mange tout and baby sweet corn, and strips of celery and cucumber.

Asparagus Cream Dip

MAKES ABOUT 300 ML/10 FL OZ

Use fresh young asparagus for this dip. It's very easy to make and tastes divine.

250 g/9 oz fresh young asparagus
125 ml/4 fl oz double cream
Freshly ground black pepper
Trimmed green beans, endive and young asparagus for dipping

1. Cut the asparagus for the dip into 2.5 cm (1 in) pieces. Place all the asparagus in a small saucepan with 150 ml/5 fl oz cold water, bring to the boil, cover and simmer for ten minutes, until just tender. Drain and refresh under cold running water. Drain well and leave to cool completely. Reserve the spears for dipping.
2. Place the cold asparagus pieces in a blender or food processor and blend for a few seconds until smooth. If necessary add one to two tablespoons of cream to help process the asparagus.
3. Lightly whip the remaining cream in a bowl, then stir in the asparagus. Season well with freshly ground black pepper. Cover and chill.
4. Spoon the dip into a serving bowl. Serve with the asparagus spears and chilled green beans, plus endive leaves. If serving this dip as a first course when entertaining, spoon into individual ramekin dishes.

Artichoke Heart Dip

MAKES ABOUT 375 ML/12 FL OZ

400 g14 oz canned artichoke hearts, well drained
200 g/7 oz cream cheese
50 ml/2 fl oz double cream
Freshly ground black pepper
Grilled vegetables, e.g. strips of red and yellow pepper,
courgettes and aubergine

1. Place the well-drained artichoke hearts, cream cheese and cream in a blender or food processor and process for a few seconds until smooth and well combined. Turn the dip into a bowl, season to taste, cover and chill.
2. Spoon the dip into a serving dish. Serve with strips of red and yellow pepper, courgette and aubergine that have been brushed with olive oil, seasoned and grilled until tender. Don't worry if some of the skins char slightly as this adds flavour.

Celery and Spinach Dip

MAKES ABOUT 375 ML/12 FL OZ

Use young leaf spinach and cut it very finely so it will blend into the dip. The crisp celery adds a light crunch. Serve this fairly thick dip with a selection of cheese crackers.

200 g/7 oz cream cheese
50 g/2 oz mayonnaise
3 Tbsp milk
1 garlic clove, crushed (optional)
2 celery stalks, finely chopped
50 g/2 oz young baby leaves of spinach
Freshly ground black pepper
Selection of small cheese crackers

1. Soften the cream cheese with the mayonnaise in a bowl. Blend in the milk and garlic, if using. Stir in the celery.
2. Wash the spinach and remove any coarse stalks. Drain well and pat dry with paper towels. Roll up small bunches of spinach leaves and cut into fine shreds with a sharp knife. Stir the shredded spinach into the dip. Season well with freshly ground black pepper. Cover and chill.
3. Turn the dip into a serving bowl. Serve with a selection of small cheese crackers.

Tomato and Onion Sambal

MAKES ABOUT 450 ML/15 FL OZ

2 large tomatoes, deseeded and finely diced
1 medium onion, finely chopped
2 Tbsp lemon juice
½ tsp cumin seeds
A good pinch cayenne pepper
Strips of pitta bread and crusty bread

1. Place the chopped tomato, onion, lemon juice, cumin seeds and cayenne into a bowl and mix thoroughly. Cover and chill.
2. Serve the sambal with traditional Indian foods such as strips of pitta bread cut wide enough to scoop up the chopped pieces of vegetables. Crusty bread is also an ideal accompaniment.

Tomato and Chilli Salsa

MAKES ABOUT 450 ML/15 FL OZ

2 large tomatoes, deseeded and finely diced
1 medium onion, finely chopped
3 green chillies, deseeded and finely chopped
2 Tbsp fresh coriander, chopped
Freshly ground black pepper
Fresh coriander leaves
Wide strips of red, yellow, green and orange peppers and
tortilla crisps

1. Place the tomato, onion, chillies and coriander in a bowl and mix thoroughly. Season well with freshly ground black pepper. Cover and chill.

2. Transfer the salsa to a serving dish and garnish with coriander leaves. Serve pieces of different coloured peppers, cut wide enough to scoop up the salsa and tortilla crisps as accompaniments.

Butternut Squash Dip

MAKES ABOUT 375 ML/15 FL OZ

Butternut squash and nutmeg have a lovely sweet and warming quality as a dip. The dip can be served warm or chilled, but I prefer it served warm with sweet potatoes cooked with their skins on, cut into wedges and fried or oven roasted. A true winter comfort food.

1 butternut squash, weighing about 675 g/1½ lb
½ tsp nutmeg, freshly grated, plus a little to serve
50 ml/2 fl oz double cream
Freshly ground black pepper
Fried or oven roasted sweet potato wedges with their skins on

1. Cut the butternut squash in half lengthwise. Scoop out the seeds. Using a sharp knife or vegetable peeler carefully remove the skin. Cut the flesh into chunks.
2. Place the cubes of squash into a saucepan with 150 ml/5 fl oz cold water and ½ tsp freshly grated nutmeg. Bring to the boil, cover, and simmer for about ten minutes, until just tender. Stir and turn the pieces of squash occasionally, so they cook evenly in the small quantity of water used. Take care not to overcook the squash.
3. Drain the cooked squash well and allow to cool slightly, then purée for a few seconds in a food processor or blender until smooth.
4. Stir in the cream, season and serve immediately or allow to cool completely, cover, and chill in the refrigerator.
5. Just before serving the dip, grate a little more nutmeg on top and serve with fried or baked sweet potato wedges.

Mushroom and Pine Nut Dip

MAKES ABOUT 300 ML/10 FL OZ

Use large, flat-open mushrooms because they have a stronger mushroom flavour than the small button variety.

4 Tbsp olive oil
250 g/9 oz large open mushrooms, finely chopped
230 g/8 oz canned tomatoes in tomato juice, drained and chopped
50 g/2 oz pine nuts
Freshly ground black pepper
1 Tbsp fresh parsley, chopped
A selection of crackers and strips of crusty bread

1. Heat the oil in a saucepan and sauté the chopped mushrooms. Cook for about ten minutes over a moderate heat so that the juices released from the mushrooms evaporate and only the olive oil and concentrated cooked mushrooms are left in the pan. Stir occasionally. Leave to cool.
2. Meanwhile, place the pine nuts in a single layer on a heatproof baking sheet and place under a hot, preheated grill. Grill for one to two minutes until the pine nuts turn a pale golden colour, turn them occasionally so they toast evenly. Take care that the pine nuts don't suddenly turn brown and burn. Remove from the heat and allow to cool.
3. Place the mushrooms and any olive oil from the pan, the tomatoes and all but one tablespoon of pine nuts in a blender or food processor. Process for a few seconds until smooth. Transfer to a bowl and season to taste. Cover and chill.
4. Spoon the dip into a serving bowl and sprinkle with the reserved pine nuts and chopped parsley. Serve with a selection of crackers and strips of crusty bread.

Creamy Corn Dip

MAKES ABOUT 375 ML/12 FL OZ

125 g/4 oz sweet corn kernels (canned or frozen)
150 ml/5 fl oz double cream
25 g/1 oz Parmesan, freshly grated
2 Tbsp mayonnaise
1 Tbsp fresh chives, chopped
Freshly ground black pepper
Cheese straws, cubed bagels, and strips of cucumber,
carrot and celery

1. If using canned sweet corn, drain it well. Alternatively, if using frozen sweet corn, cook in boiling water, drain and cool completely. Reserve a tablespoon of sweet corn for garnish.

2. Lightly whip the cream and stir in the remaining sweet corn, Parmesan, mayonnaise and chives. Season to taste with freshly ground black pepper. Cover and chill.

3. Spoon the dip into a serving bowl and sprinkle with the reserved sweet corn. Serve with cheese straws, cubed bagels, and strips of cucumber, carrot and celery.

Cucumber and Lime Raita

MAKES ABOUT 300 ML/10 FL OZ

½ cucumber (18 cm/7 in)
150 g/5 oz natural yogurt
1 garlic clove, crushed
2 Tbsp celery leaves, finely chopped
1 lime, juice, and rind finely grated
Freshly ground black pepper
Celery leaves
Strips of warm pitta bread, cubes of crusty bread and
strips of cucumber and celery

1. Peel the cucumber, cut in half lengthwise. Using a teaspoon, scoop out the seeds. Coarsely grate the cucumber flesh into a bowl. Drain any excess liquid collected in the bowl from the grated cucumber.

2. Add the yogurt, garlic, celery leaves, lime juice and rind, mixing thoroughly. Season to taste with freshly ground black pepper. Cover and chill.

3. Transfer the raita to a serving dish and garnish with celery leaves. Serve with strips of warm pitta bread, cubes of crusty bread and strips of cucumber and celery.

Tapenade

MAKES ABOUT 300 ML/10 FL OZ

200 g/7 oz pitted black olives
1 Tbsp capers, drained
1 garlic clove, crushed
2 tsp Dijon mustard
2 tsp lemon juice
125 ml/4 fl oz olive oil
Freshly ground black pepper
Toasted crusty bread slices and olive bread

1. Reserve a couple of olives for a garnish. Place the remaining olives, capers, garlic, mustard and lemon juice in a blender or food processor and process for a few seconds until smooth.

2. Add the olive oil *gradually* through the hole in the lid while the blender or processor is running. The oil must be added gradually so that the mixture is well emulsified and smooth. Turn the tapenade into a bowl and season with freshly ground black pepper. Cover and chill for at least two hours to let the flavours develop.

3. Spoon the tapenade into a serving bowl and garnish with reserved olives. Serve with toasted crusty bread and olive bread if available.

BEAN AND LENTIL DIPS

5

Hummus

MAKES ABOUT 375 ML/12 FL OZ

Although this dip can be processed until smooth, I prefer to leave it quite chunky so that the chickpeas give it some texture and bite. Enjoy the dip as a light lunch or at parties.

1 Tbsp sesame seeds
430 g/15 oz canned chickpeas, drained
3 garlic cloves, crushed
3 Tbsp olive oil
3 Tbsp lemon juice
Freshly ground black pepper
Sprig of fresh parsley
Strips of warm pitta bread, and peppers, celery and cucumber

1. Place the sesame seeds in a single layer on a piece of aluminium foil on a baking tray. Place under a moderately hot preheated grill for about two to three minutes, until they are lightly toasted. Take care that they don't burn. Stir the sesame seeds occasionally so that they turn an even golden brown.

2. Place the sesame seeds, chickpeas, garlic, olive oil and lemon juice in a blender or food processor and process for a few seconds until combined, but not too smooth. Transfer the hummus to a bowl and season to taste with freshly ground black pepper. Cover and chill.

3. Spoon the hummus into a serving dish and garnish with a sprig of parsley. Serve with strips of warm pitta bread and peppers, celery and cucumber.

Red Lentil Dhal

MAKES ABOUT 450 ML/15 FL OZ

This mildly spiced dhal makes an ideal dip for a packed lunch or a first course before a curry main meal.

1 Tbsp sunflower oil
1 medium onion, finely chopped
2 garlic cloves, crushed
2.5 cm/1 in piece fresh root ginger, peeled and finely chopped
1 tsp ground coriander
1 tsp ground cumin
1 tsp ground turmeric
175 g/6 oz dried red lentils
Chilli powder
Strips of warm pitta bread, crusty bread and strips of celery and cucumber

1. Heat the oil in a saucepan and sauté the onion, garlic, ginger and spices over a moderate heat for three minutes, stirring occasionally and taking care not to burn the spices.

2. Add the red lentils and 600 ml/1 pt cold water. Bring to the boil and cook rapidly for ten minutes. Cover and simmer for another fifteen to twenty minutes, or until the lentils are tender. Drain well and leave to cool completely.

3. Place three-quarters of the lentil mixture into a blender or food processor and process for a few seconds, until smooth. Turn into a bowl and stir in the remaining lentils to give the dip some texture. Cover and chill.

4. Transfer the dhal to a serving dish and sprinkle with a pinch of chilli powder to garnish. Serve with strips of warm pitta bread, crusty bread and strips of celery and cucumber.

Hot Tex Mex Dip

MAKES ABOUT 300 ML/10 FL OZ

This hearty, colourful Mexican dip is a real feast. If you prefer your chilli flavour really hot, then there is no need to deseed the chillies before chopping.

225 g/8 oz canned kidney beans, drained and rinsed
225 g/8 oz canned tomatoes, drained and chopped
2 green chillies, deseeded and chopped
3 Tbsp onion, finely chopped
½ small yellow pepper, deseeded and finely diced
½ small green pepper, deseeded and finely diced
Chunky strips of pepper, tortilla crisps and taco shells

1. Combine the kidney beans, tomatoes, chillies, onion and yellow and green pepper. Cover and chill.

2. Transfer the dip into a serving bowl. Serve with strips of yellow, green and red pepper cut wide enough to scoop up the chunky dip. Tortilla crisps and taco shells are also suitable accompaniments.

Green Lentil and Spinach Dip

MAKES ABOUT 375 ML/12 FL OZ

125 g/4 oz dried green lentils, rinsed and drained
125 g/4 oz fresh young spinach, washed and drained
150 g/5 oz natural yogurt
2 tsp hot curry powder
Chunky strips of pitta bread and peppers

1. Place the lentils in a saucepan with 600 ml/1 pt cold water. Bring to the boil and cook rapidly for ten minutes. Cover and simmer for another fifteen to twenty minutes, or until tender. Drain and allow to cool completely.
2. Meanwhile, place the spinach in a large heatproof colander over a sink and pour over 1¼ l/2 pt boiling water – this is all the cooking the spinach will require. Drain well and allow to cool completely. When the spinach is cool, squeeze out any excess water and cut it into fine shreds.
3. Blend the yogurt and curry powder together in a bowl. Stir in the cold lentils and spinach. Cover and chill.
4. Transfer the lentil dip into a serving bowl and serve with chunky pieces of pitta bread and peppers to scoop up this hearty dip.

Curried Bean Dip

MAKES ABOUT 375 ML/12 FL OZ

420 g/15 oz canned mixed beans, e.g. chickpeas, pinto, black-eyed, kidney, drained and rinsed
125 g/4 oz natural yogurt
1 tsp hot curry powder
1 tsp lemon juice
Slices of lemon and a pinch of curry powder
Strips of warm pitta bread and crusty bread

1. Blend the yogurt, curry powder and lemon juice together. Stir in the beans. Cover and chill.
2. Transfer the dip to a serving bowl. Garnish with slices of lemon and sprinkle with the pinch of curry powder. Serve with wide strips of warm pitta bread and crusty bread to scoop up this chunky dip.

Butter Bean Dip

MAKES ABOUT 300 ML/10 FL OZ

Butter beans have a creamy flavour that go well with fish to make a filling meal. Or, serve with vegetables as a lighter alternative.

420 g/15 oz canned butter beans, drained and rinsed
75 g/3 oz natural yogurt
½ small lemon, juice, and rind finely grated
2 Tbsp fresh parsley, chopped
Freshly ground black pepper
Baked or fried batter-coated fish nuggets or scampi
AND/OR strips of carrot, broccoli florets and blanched green beans

1. Place the butter beans and yogurt in a blender or food processor and process for a few seconds until smooth. Transfer the bean purée to a bowl.
2. Stir in the lemon juice and rind and parsley. Season well with freshly ground black pepper. Cover and chill.
3. Spoon the dip into a serving bowl and serve with warm, cooked batter-coated fish sticks for a substantial dip, or alternatively serve a selection of vegetables such as strips of carrot, broccoli florets and blanched green beans.

Pesto Bean Dip

MAKES ABOUT 300 ML/10 FL OZ

Pesto sauce can be bought ready-made and has
a distinctive basil flavour.

2 Tbsp pesto
425 g/15 oz canned soya beans, drained and rinsed
75 g/3 oz natural yogurt
Tomato wedges, breadsticks, crusty bread and olive bread,
cubed

1. Place the pesto, beans and yogurt in a blender
or food processor and process for a few seconds
until smooth. Transfer to a bowl, cover and chill.
2. Spoon the dip into a serving bowl and serve
with wedges of tomato, breadsticks and cubes of
crusty and olive bread.

Mexican Bean Dip

MAKES ABOUT 300 ML/10 FL OZ

425 g/15 oz canned red pinto beans, drained and rinsed
2 garlic cloves, crushed
3 Tbsp chopped onion
¼ tsp ground cumin
2 Tbsp olive oil
2 green chillies, deseeded and finely chopped
Strips of red, yellow, and green peppers,
and tortilla crisps

1. Place the beans, garlic, onion, cumin and olive
oil in a blender or food processor and process for a
few seconds until smooth. Transfer to a bowl and
stir in the chopped chillies. Cover and chill.
2. Spoon the dip into a serving bowl and serve
with strips of red, yellow and green peppers and
tortilla crisps.

Creamed Chickpea and Hazelnut Dip

MAKES ABOUT 375 ML/12 FL OZ

Crunchy toasted hazelnut in creamy chickpeas
makes an unusual and appetizing dip that is
popular with vegetarians as a packed lunch or
when served at a dinner party.

50 g/2 oz hazelnuts, chopped
420 g/15 oz canned chickpeas, drained and rinsed
150 ml/5 fl oz double cream
2 Tbsp milk
Freshly ground black pepper
Cored apple wedges, strips of celery and cucumber
and potato crisps

1. Place the chopped hazelnuts in a single layer
on a sheet of aluminium foil on a baking tray.
Toast under a moderate, preheated grill for about
two to three minutes, turning occasionally, until
they turn a golden brown. Take care that they
don't brown too suddenly. Remove from the heat
and leave to cool completely.
2. Place the chickpeas, cream and milk in a
blender or food processor and process for a few
seconds until smooth.
3. Turn the chickpea mixture into a bowl. Reserve
one tablespoon of the toasted hazelnuts and stir
the remaining nuts into the chickpea mixture.
Season well with freshly ground black pepper.
Cover and chill.
4. Spoon the dip into a serving bowl and sprinkle
with the reserved hazelnuts. Serve with cored
apple wedges (dipped in lemon juice to prevent
discolouring), strips of celery and cucumber and
potato crisps.

FRUIT DIPS –
6
SAVOURY AND SWEET

Cranberry and Orange Dip with Herbed Crumb-coated Turkey Sticks

MAKES ABOUT 450 ML/15 FL OZ

Christmas and Thanksgiving are ideal occasions for serving this festive dip with strips of turkey coated in parsley- and thyme-flavoured bread crumbs for added crunch and flavour.

FOR THE DIP
400 g/14 oz cranberries
2 large oranges, juice and rind, finely grated
3 oz caster sugar
Salt and freshly ground black pepper

FOR THE TURKEY STICKS
450 g/1 lb skinless and boneless turkey breast meat
2 eggs, beaten
175 g/6 oz dried breadcrumb stuffing mix,
e.g. parsley and thyme
Vegetable oil for deep frying

1. Place the cranberries, orange juice and 50 ml/ 2 fl oz cold water in a large saucepan. Reserve one teaspoon of the orange rind for a garnish and add the remaining rind to the cranberries. *Slowly* bring to the boil, cover, and simmer for about fifteen to twenty minutes, until the cranberries are tender. As the cranberries come to the boil, take care not to get burned by hot cranberry juice. This can be reduced by heating slowly.

2. Remove the cooked cranberries from the heat. Stir in the sugar until it has dissolved completely. Allow the dip to cool.

3. Pour the cranberry mixture into a blender or

food processor and process for a few seconds until smooth. Spoon the purée into a fine nylon sieve over a bowl and press through the purée to remove the cranberry skins. Season to taste, and cover the sieved cranberry dip and chill.

4. To make the Turkey Sticks: Cut the turkey breast meat into 1 cm by 5 cm (½ in by 2 in) strips. Dip the turkey strips, a few at a time, into the beaten eggs and then into the herbed breadcrumb mixture. Deep fry, in batches, in oil preheated to 180°C/355°F for about five minutes or until the crumbs are golden and crisp and the turkey is thoroughly cooked. Drain on paper towels and keep warm while cooking the remaining batches.

5. Transfer the dip to a serving dish and sprinkle with the reserved orange rind. Serve with the warm turkey sticks.

Apricot and Mango Chutney Dip

MAKES ABOUT 375 ML/12 FL OZ

Serve this dip with warm samosas and onion rings for a real feast.

200 g/7 oz dried apricots
5 whole green cardamoms
3 Tbsp mango chutney
Samosas and onion rings

1. Place the dried apricots in a large bowl and cover with 600 ml/1 pt cold water. Leave to soak overnight.

2. Place the soaked apricots in a saucepan with the soaking water and green cardamoms. Bring to the boil, cover and simmer for forty minutes.

Allow the cooked apricots to cool completely in the liquid.

3. Drain the apricots. Remove the cardamoms. Place the apricots in a blender or food processor and process for a few seconds until smooth.

4. Transfer the apricot purée to a bowl and stir in the mango chutney. Cover and chill.

5. Transfer the dip to a serving bowl and serve with samosas and onion rings.

Pineapple, Avocado and Red Onion Salsa

MAKES ABOUT 450 ML/15 FL OZ

225 g/8 oz canned pineapple in natural juice
1 red onion, finely chopped
1 green chilli, deseeded and chopped
1 medium avocado
2 Tbsp fresh coriander, chopped
Freshly ground black pepper
Tortilla crisps, nachos and pitta bread cut into wide strips

1. Drain the pineapple, reserving the juice. Chop the pineapple into small pieces.

2. Cut the avocado in half lengthwise and twist the halves in opposite directions to pull the two halves apart. Remove the stone and skin. Finely dice the avocado flesh and toss in the reserved pineapple juice to prevent discolouration.

3. Combine all of the ingredients in a bowl and season well with freshly ground black pepper. Cover and chill.

4. Transfer the salsa to a serving dish and serve with tortilla crisps, nachos and pitta bread cut in strips wide enough so that the chunky salsa can be scooped up.

Pineapple and Chive Cheese Dip

MAKES ABOUT 300 ML/10 FL OZ

The hollowed-out pineapple shells make ideal containers in which to serve this dip. It's best to serve it fairly soon after making; on standing the fresh pineapple exudes juice that can make the dip too moist.

1 small, ripe pineapple
125 g/4 oz cottage cheese
2 Tbsp natural yogurt
2 Tbsp fresh chives, chopped
Pinch of paprika
Freshly ground black pepper
Fresh chives, chopped
A selection of crackers, strips of celery, cucumber and carrot

1. Cut the pineapple in half lengthwise. With a sharp knife carefully cut around the inner edge of the pineapple halves and scoop out the flesh with a spoon.

2. Place the empty pineapple halves upside down on a deep plate to allow excess juice to run out. Cover and chill.

3. Cut the pineapple flesh into small chunks. Place the pieces in a sieve over a bowl and allow any excess juice to drain away.

4. Combine the cottage cheese with the yogurt in a bowl. Stir in the pineapple chunks, chives and paprika. Season to taste with freshly ground black pepper. Cover and chill.

5. Just before serving, spoon the dip into the pineapple halves and garnish with chopped chives. Serve with a selection of crackers and strips of celery, cucumber and carrot.

Curried Mango Dip

MAKES ABOUT 375 ML/12 FL OZ

Mango and Indian spices make an unusual and
tasty dip, which never fails to impress.

1 medium, ripe mango (you require about 200 g/7 oz flesh)
2 Tbsp mango chutney
1 tsp medium hot curry paste OR ½ tsp medium hot curry
powder
125 g/4 oz natural yogurt
Fresh sprigs of coriander
Crusty bread, pitta bread cut into strips; cucumber and red
pepper strips

1. Cut down either side of the large, flat mango
stone with a sharp knife to remove the flesh.
Using a vegetable peeler or sharp knife, remove
the mango skin. Roughly chop the mango and
place in a blender or food processor and process
for a few seconds until smooth.
2. Turn the mango purée into a mixing bowl and
stir in the mango chutney, curry paste or powder
and yogurt. Cover and chill.
3. Transfer the dip to a serving dish and garnish
with fresh coriander leaves. Serve with a selection
of crusty breads, strips of pitta bread, cucumber
and red pepper.

Paw-paw, Mango and Pomegranate Salsa

MAKES ABOUT 450 ML/15 FL OZ

This chunky, colourful salsa wakes up tired taste
buds with its fruity and fiery flavours.

1 small, ripe mango
1 medium, ripe paw-paw
1 pomegranate
1 small onion, finely chopped
2 green chillies, deseeded and finely chopped
1 Tbsp fresh coriander, chopped
Freshly ground black pepper
Tortilla crisps and wide strips of red, yellow and green
peppers

1. Cut down each side of the large, central stone
in the mango with a sharp knife to remove the
flesh. With a vegetable peeler or sharp knife,
remove the mango skin. Finely dice the mango
and place in a bowl.
2. Prepare the paw-paw by cutting in half
lengthwise and scooping out the black seeds with
a spoon. Remove the skin with a vegetable peeler
or sharp knife. Cut the pawpaw flesh into finely
diced pieces and add to the mango.
3. Lightly roll the pomegranate with your hand
on a kitchen surface to loosen the fruit inside. Cut
the pomegranate in half and carefully pick out the
pieces of pomegranate from the husk and add to
the mango and pawpaw.
4. Add the prepared onion, chillies and coriander
to the fruit and mix thoroughly. Season well with
freshly ground black pepper. Cover and chill.
5. Transfer the salsa to a serving dish. Serve with
foods suitable for scooping up the chunky texture
of the salsa, such as tortilla crisps and wide strips
of red, yellow and green peppers.

Kiwi Cream Dip

MAKES ABOUT 375 ML/12 FL OZ

3 ripe kiwis
1 Tbsp apricot brandy
150 g/5 oz natural yogurt
Small wedges of peeled mango, paw-paw and banana

1. Trim off the ends of the kiwis and remove the skin with a sharp knife or vegetable peeler. Reserve a few slices for decoration and roughly chop the remaining fruit. Place in a blender or food processor and process until smooth.
2. Pour the purée into a bowl and stir in the apricot brandy. Lightly swirl in the yogurt. Cover and chill.
3. To serve, decorate with the reserved kiwi slices. Serve with small wedges of peeled mango, paw-paw and banana (dipped in lime juice to prevent discolouring).

Strawberry Dream Dip

MAKES ABOUT 300 ML/10 FL OZ

150 g/5 oz strawberries, hulled
2 Tbsp icing sugar
200 g/7 oz natural yogurt
Wedges of pear, peach and banana OR marshmallows, mini doughnuts and mini sweet muffins

1. Place the strawberries in a small processor or blender and process for a few seconds until smooth. Transfer the purée to a fine nylon sieve set over a small bowl and with a spoon or press the purée through the sieve to remove the seeds.
2. Stir the icing sugar into the strawberry purée and then blend in the yogurt until smooth. Cover and chill.

3. Turn the dip into a serving dish. For health-conscious diners, serve with wedges of cored pear, peach and banana (coated in lime or lemon juice to prevent discolouring), or, for a more wicked feast, try dipping marshmallows, mini doughnuts, and mini sweet muffins. Delicious!

Blueberry Swirl Dip

MAKES ABOUT 300 ML/10 FL OZ

Serve this dip soon after lightly swirling the blueberries and yogurt together or else the blueberry colour "bleeds" into the white and the dip's stunning appearance is lost (although it still tastes as good!)

250 g/9 oz blueberries, fresh or frozen
2 tsp arrowroot
75 g/3 oz natural yogurt
Peeled and cored pear wedges, and chocolate and vanilla sponge cake

1. Place the blueberries in a saucepan with 75 ml/ 3 fl oz cold water. Bring to the boil and simmer for five minutes, until tender.
2. Blend the arrowroot in a small cup with two tablespoons cold water. Stir one tablespoon of the hot blueberry liquid into the arrowroot, then pour the blended mixture into the blueberries and stir well. Return to the boil, stirring continuously until thickened (this should only take seconds). Remove the pan from the heat and allow to cool completely. Chill in the refrigerator until just about to serve.
3. Pour the blueberry mixture into a serving bowl and lightly swirl in the yogurt. Serve with peeled and cored wedges of pear (which have been dipped in lemon juice to prevent discolouring) and chocolate and vanilla sponge cake cut into cubes.

Cinnamon and Raisin Yogurt Dip with Apple Fritters

MAKES ABOUT 300 ML/10 FL OZ

Serve this dip with warm apple fritters for best effect, but if you don't have time to make them then wedges of cored apple can be served instead. Calvados is a brandy made from apples – if you don't have any, use cider or apple juice to plump up the raisins.

FOR THE DIP
75 g/3 oz raisins
3 Tbsp Calvados
225 g/8 oz natural yogurt
½ tsp ground cinnamon

FOR THE APPLE FRITTERS
1 quantity of batter (see Quick Tomato Dip with Turkey Sticks, page 28 for batter recipe)
5 large eating apples
Vegetable oil, for deep frying
Dusting of icing sugar, for dredging over cooked apple fritters

1. To make the Dip: In a small bowl, soak the raisins in the Calvados for at least two hours or preferably overnight. Then combine all of the dip ingredients, cover and chill.

2. To make the Apple Fritters: Heat the oil for frying to 190°C/375°F. Peel and core the apples. Cut the apples into rings about 5 mm (¼ in) thick. When the oil is up to temperature, dip the apple rings into the batter, shake off the excess and carefully place them in the hot oil. Cook a few at a time, turning them over when one side is golden brown. When completely golden, remove with a slotted spoon and drain on paper towels. Keep warm while cooking the remaining apple rings.

3. Dredge the warm apple fritters with icing sugar and serve immediately with the dip.

Autumnal Fruits with Port Dip

MAKES ABOUT 450 ML/15 FL OZ

There is something warming and comforting about this dip – its rich, luscious colours and indescribable flavour make you go back for more and more. While it can be served warm or chilled, I like to serve it warm at bonfire night parties. Make sure you have plenty of dipping accompaniments to serve with it.

300 g/11 oz mixed berries, e.g. redcurrants, blackcurrants, raspberries, blackberries (fresh or frozen)
150 ml/5 fl oz port
3 Tbsp caster sugar
4 tsp arrowroot
Cored apple wedges, mini sweet muffins, sponge fingers and marshmallows

1. Place the berries in a saucepan with 75 ml/ 3 fl oz of the port and the sugar. Bring to the boil and simmer uncovered for ten minutes.
2. Blend the arrowroot with the remaining port. Add two tablespoons of the hot berry mixture to the blended arrowroot, then pour the mixture back into the saucepan. Return to the boil, stirring continuously, until thickened.
3. If serving hot, pour into a heatproof serving dish immediately, or allow to cool completely, then cover and chill in the refrigerator until required. Serve the dip with apples cored and cut into wedges (dipped in lemon juice to prevent discolouring), mini sweet muffins, sponge fingers and marshmallows.

Butterscotch Dip with Grilled Bananas

MAKES ABOUT 250 ML/8 FL OZ
SERVES 4 PEOPLE AS A DESSERT

This dip is extremely sweet but delicious. It's a dip that has to be served warm and I particularly like to serve it with banana slices that have been warmed under the grill.

150 g/5 oz pourable honey
6 Tbsp butter
50 g/2 oz dark brown sugar
4 large bananas, ripe but firm
Juice of 1 lemon

1. Place the honey, butter and brown sugar in a small saucepan and heat very gently, stirring occasionally until the butter and sugar have completely dissolved in the honey. Take care not to boil the mixture. Keep it on a low heat to stay warm while the bananas are prepared.
2. Peel the bananas and cut in half lengthwise. Cut each half of the banana into thirds and dip in the lemon juice. Place the banana pieces under a hot preheated grill for just long enough to warm them through – only a couple of minutes. Take care not to cook them too long or they suddenly go soft and then can't be dipped into the Butterscotch Dip. (If this does happen then never fear, the dip can be served poured over the bananas – as I have done a few times when I've been too busy chatting with my guests!)
3. Serve the butterscotch dip in individual ramekins placed on a plate with the grilled bananas arranged around the side.

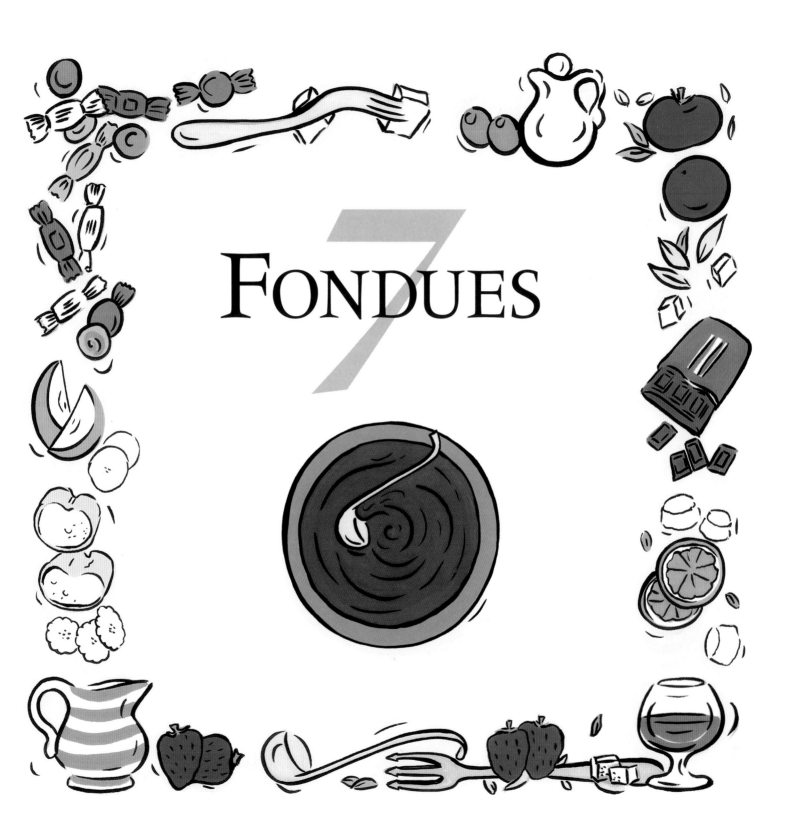

7 FONDUES

Fondues are often considered the ultimate dips – they are always served warm and often contain alcohol.

They are great dips for an informal meal or supper with friends when you can sit and chat, relaxing and idly dipping into the fondue. It has been said that fondues make ideal party food, since if a person drops a piece of food from their fork into the fondue, they then have to carry out a forfeit – I'll leave those forfeit suggestions to your imagination. Whenever you have your fondue, simply have fun and enjoy.

Don't worry if you haven't got a fondue set, you can still keep your fondue warm by pouring it into a warmed heatproof dish over a tabletop warmer with nightlights. Long-handled fondue forks do help with the dipping, but ordinary forks or skewers can be used as an alternative.

The savoury fondues in this chapter make about 600 ml/1 pt, which will serve six to eight people for a first course or four people as a main course when accompanied with plenty of dipping foods.

The sweet fondues make about 300 ml/ 10 fl oz, which should serve four to six people as a dessert, since they are very rich. However, if you fancy a sweet dip with no other courses, then double up the ingredients.

The secret to successful fondues is the very slow melting of the ingredients over a very low heat, so that they combine thoroughly without separating or burning on the base of the pan. Be patient – don't rush this stage and you will be rewarded with a beautifully smooth fondue dip. Also warm the serving dish in which you will serve the fondue, especially for the cheese fondues: If they cool the cheese starts to reset and becomes too thick and stringy for dipping. However, if this does occur, do not fear; just gently reheat the fondue mixture.

Cider and Cheese Fondue

MAKES ABOUT 600 ML/1 PT

350 g/12 oz Gruyère cheese, finely grated
1 garlic clove, crushed
250 ml/8 fl oz plus 15 ml/1 Tbsp medium dry cider
1 Tbsp cornflour
Freshly ground black pepper
Cored wedges of apple, cubes of crusty bread,
strips of cooked ham, chunks of cucumber and celery
and tomato wedges

1. Place the cheese, garlic and 250 ml/8 fl oz of the cider in a heavy-based saucepan and heat very gently, until the cheese has completely melted into the cider – this will take about twenty minutes. Stir the mixture occasionally.

2. When the cheese has melted, in a bowl blend the cornflour with the remaining cider and add two tablespoons of the hot fondue mixture. Immediately return the mixture to the pan and stir well. Season well with freshly ground black pepper.

3. Pour the fondue into a warmed, heatproof serving dish. Keep the fondue warm over a fondue holder or tabletop warmer with nightlights. Serve with plenty of dipping accompaniments such as cored apple wedges (dipped in lemon juice to prevent discolouring), cubes of crusty bread, strips of cooked ham, chunks of celery and cucumber and tomato wedges.

Double Cheese Fondue

MAKES ABOUT 600 ML/1 PT

175 g/6 oz Gruyère cheese, finely grated
175 g/6 oz Emmanthal cheese, finely grated
250 ml/8 fl oz plus 1 Tbsp dry white wine
1 Tbsp cornflour
Freshly ground black pepper
Cubes of crusty bread, small breadsticks, cheese straws,
diced peppers, tomato wedges and sliced courgettes

1. Place the cheeses and 250 ml/8 fl oz of the wine into a heavy-based saucepan and heat very gently, until the cheese has completely melted into the wine – this will take about twenty minutes. Stir the mixture occasionally.

2. When the cheese has melted, in a bowl blend the cornflour with the remaining wine, add two tablespoons of the hot fondue, and immediately return the mixture to the pan, stirring thoroughly. Season well with freshly ground black pepper.

3. Pour the fondue into a warmed, heatproof serving dish and place over a fondue holder or tabletop warmer with nightlights. Serve with plenty of dipping accompaniments such as cubed crusty bread, breadsticks, cheese straws, diced peppers, tomato wedges and slices of raw courgette.

Devil's Chocolate Fondue

MAKES ABOUT 300 ML/10 FL OZ

200 g/7 oz milk chocolate, broken into small cubes
4 Tbsp butter
50 ml/2 fl oz milk
3 Tbsp brandy
Cubes of sponge cake, mini sweet muffins,
mini doughnuts and biscuits

1. Place the chocolate, butter and milk in a small, heavy-based saucepan and heat very gently, until the ingredients have completely melted and combined thoroughly – this will take about fifteen minutes. Stir occasionally.

2. Stir in the brandy. Pour into a warmed, heatproof serving dish and keep warm over a fondue holder or a tabletop warmer with nightlights. Serve with cubed pieces of sponge cake, mini sweet muffins, mini doughnuts and biscuits for dipping.

Marshmallow Delight Fondue

MAKES ABOUT 300 ML/10 FL OZ

200 g/7 oz mini white marshmallows
75 g/3 oz condensed milk
2 Tbsp milk
Seedless grapes, sliced bananas and peaches
and strawberries

1. Place the marshmallows, condensed milk and milk into a small, heavy-based saucepan and heat very slowly, until the marshmallows have completely melted and combined with the other ingredients. This will take about fifteen to twenty minutes – a very low heat is required to prevent the marshmallow from burning on the base of the pan. Stir the mixture occasionally.

2. Pour the marshmallow fondue into a warmed, heatproof serving dish and keep warm over a fondue holder or a tabletop warmer with nightlights. Serve with seedless grapes, sliced bananas and peaches (both dipped in lemon juice to prevent discolouring), and strawberries for dipping.

Fresh Tomato and Basil Fondue

MAKES ABOUT 600 ML/1 PT

1 kg/2 lb large, ripe tomatoes
1 Tbsp olive oil
1 small onion, finely chopped
1 garlic clove, crushed
75 ml/3 fl oz dry white wine
1 tsp caster sugar
Freshly ground black pepper
2 Tbsp fresh basil, chopped
Cubed crusty garlic bread, shelled, cooked jumbo prawns,
diced peppers and chunks of celery

1. Skin the tomatoes by cutting a small cross in the base of each tomato with a sharp knife then place them in a heatproof bowl and pour over boiling water. Leave for a few seconds and you should see the skins loosen and start to peel away. Drain in a colander and cool under cold running water. Remove the skins, then chop the tomatoes into wedges and discard the seeds. Finely chop the remaining tomato flesh.
2. Heat the oil in a saucepan and gently sauté the onion and garlic for five minutes, until softened but not browned.
3. Add the chopped tomato and slowly bring to a boil. Simmer, uncovered, for about twenty to thirty minutes so that the tomato mixture can reduce and thicken.
4. Remove from the heat, stir in the wine and sugar. Season to taste with freshly ground black pepper. Pour the tomato fondue into a warmed heatproof serving dish and keep warm over a fondue holder or on a tabletop warmer with nightlights. Sprinkle with the chopped basil. Serve with plenty of dipping accompaniments such as cubed crusty garlic bread, shelled, cooked jumbo prawns, diced peppers and chunks of celery.

Creamy Toffee Fondue with Popcorn

MAKES ABOUT 300 ML/10 FL OZ

Use creamy toffee rather than a brittle toffee when making this fondue.

200 g/7 oz creamy toffees
4 Tbsp butter
50 ml/2 fl oz milk
Plain unsalted or unsweetened popcorn

1. Place the toffees, butter and milk in a small, heavy-based saucepan and heat very gently until the ingredients have completely melted and combined thoroughly – this will take about fifteen minutes. Stir the mixture occasionally.
2. Carefully pour the very hot toffee fondue into a warmed, heatproof serving dish and keep warm over a fondue holder or tabletop warmer with nightlights. Serve with freshly made, warm, unsalted, and unsweetened popcorn, using cocktail sticks to dip the popcorn into the toffee fondue.

MORE
FAVOURITES

8

Peppery Mayonnaise Dip

MAKES ABOUT 300 ML/10 FL OZ

250 g/9 oz mayonnaise
4 shallots, finely chopped
2 Tbsp fresh chives, finely chopped
2 Tbsp white whole peppercorns
Chilli sauce
Strips of celery, carrot, cucumber, courgette and blanched baby sweet corn

1. Mix together the mayonnaise, shallots and chives in a bowl.
2. Lightly crush the peppercorns in a pestle and mortar, or place in a small plastic bag and crush lightly with a rolling pin. Stir the peppercorns into the dip mixture.
3. Add as many drops of chilli sauce as your taste prefers. Five to six drops are recommended, since the flavour matures and seems to strengthen upon chilling the dip. Cover and chill.
4. Spoon the dip into a serving bowl. Serve with strips of raw celery, carrot, cucumber, courgette, and blanched and cooled baby sweet corn.

Caper and Gherkin Dip

MAKES ABOUT 375 ML/12 FL OZ

200 g/7 oz low-fat natural yogurt
2 Tbsp capers, finely chopped
75 g/3 oz pickled gherkins, finely chopped
2 Tbsp fresh tarragon, finely chopped
Freshly ground black pepper
Fresh tarragon sprigs
Strips of red, yellow and green peppers, courgette and celery

1. Combine the yogurt, capers, gherkins and tarragon. Season well with freshly ground black pepper. Cover and chill.
2. Transfer the dip to a serving dish and garnish with sprigs of tarragon. Serve with strips of red, yellow and green peppers, courgette and celery.

Wholegrain Mustard Dip

MAKES ABOUT 300 ML/10 FL OZ

200 g/7 oz mayonnaise
75 g/3 oz natural yogurt
3 Tbsp wholegrain OR coarsegrain mustard
1 tsp English mustard
Freshly ground black pepper
Deep-fried or baked batter-coated vegetables, e.g. onion rings, and strips of aubergine and courgettes

1. Place the mayonnaise, yogurt and mustards in a bowl and mix thoroughly. Season to taste with freshly ground black pepper. Cover and chill.
2. Spoon the dip into a serving dish and serve with warm deep-fried or baked chunks of batter-coated mixed vegetables, such as onion rings, and strips of aubergine and courgettes.

Egg and Parsley Dip

MAKES ABOUT 375 ML/12 FL OZ

3 hard-boiled eggs, chilled and shelled
150 g/5 oz mayonnaise
1 Tbsp milk
5 Tbsp fresh parsley, finely chopped
Freshly ground black pepper
Sprig of fresh parsley
Strips of white and brown bread, toasted

1. Place the hard-boiled eggs in a bowl and with the back of a fork mash them into fine pieces.
2. Stir thoroughly the mayonnaise and milk into the eggs. Add the fresh parsley and season well with freshly ground black pepper. Cover and chill.
3. Spoon the dip into a serving bowl and garnish with a sprig of fresh parsley. Serve with toasted strips of white and brown bread.

Fresh Herbed Yogurt Dip

MAKES ABOUT 300 ML/10 FL OZ

225 g/8 oz full-fat natural yogurt
50 g/2 oz mixed fresh herbs, e.g. chives, parsley, oregano, thyme and marjoram
Freshly ground black pepper
Fish, meat and vegetable kebabs, barbecued or grilled, and a selection of vegetable crudités

1. Place the yogurt in a bowl.
2. Remove any large or woody stalks from the herbs and chop the leaves finely. Add to the yogurt and mix thoroughly. Season well with freshly ground black pepper. Cover and chill.
3. Transfer the dip to a serving bowl. Serve with kebabs, fish, meat and vegetables (barbecued or grilled), and a selection of vegetable crudités.

Tofu and Peanut Butter Dip

125 g/4 oz smooth peanut butter
75 ml/3 fl oz milk
200 g/7 oz firm tofu, drained
1 tsp tomato paste
Cayenne pepper
2 Tbsp roasted peanuts, chopped
Toasted strips of bread and peppers

1. Place the peanut butter in a bowl. In a small saucepan, gently heat the milk until warm but not boiling. Gradually blend the milk into the peanut butter to make a smooth soft paste – I find this is best done with a fork. Allow to cool.

2. Place the tofu in a separate bowl with the tomato paste and with a fork blend together. The tofu will readily break up into a smooth mash.

3. Combine the peanut butter and tofu mixtures and season to taste with cayenne pepper. Remember cayenne is very hot, so add sparingly. Cover and chill.

4. Spoon the dip into a serving bowl and sprinkle with the chopped peanuts. Serve with strips of toasted bread and peppers.

Tofu and Sesame Dip

MAKES ABOUT 300 ML/10 FL OZ

Tofu or solid bean curd can be found in health food stores and most supermarkets. Before using tofu, drain away the excess liquid it is packed in. Tahini, also found in health food stores, has a strong sesame flavour.

1 Tbsp sesame seeds
300 g/11 oz firm tofu, drained
1 Tbsp lemon juice
1 Tbsp light tahini
1 tsp sesame oil
1 garlic clove, crushed
1 tsp cider vinegar
2 spring onions, finely chopped
Strips of celery, cucumber, peppers and carrot; small florets of broccoli and cauliflower

1. Place the sesame seeds in a single layer on a piece of aluminium foil on a baking tray. Toast under a moderate preheated grill for about two to three minutes, turning occasionally, until they turn a pale golden brown. Take care that the seeds don't brown too suddenly. Remove from the heat and allow to cool completely.

2. Place the tofu, lemon juice, tahini, sesame oil, garlic and vinegar in a blender or food processor and process for a few seconds, until smooth. Transfer to a bowl and stir in three-quarters of the chopped spring onions. Reserve the remaining spring onions as a garnish. Cover and chill.

3. Transfer the dip to a serving bowl and sprinkle with the sesame seeds and reserved chopped spring onion. Serve with strips of celery, cucumber, bell peppers and carrot and small florets of broccoli and cauliflower.

Creamy Egg Brunch Dip

MAKES ABOUT 450 ML/15 FL OZ

This delicious dip makes an ideal brunch on weekends when you have visiting guests and could also be served at a "working breakfast" where it's bound to impress! Serves four to six when accompanied with plenty of cooked cocktail sausages, bacon strips, smoked salmon rolled up into bite sized pieces and tomato wedges. Serve also with toast, warm crusty bread and plenty of coffee or tea.

6 eggs
150 ml/5 fl oz double cream
Salt and freshly ground black pepper
2 Tbsp butter
2 Tbsp fresh chives, chopped
Cooked cocktail sausages, fried bacon strips, thinly sliced smoked salmon (cut and rolled up), tomato wedges, toast and crusty bread

1. Beat the eggs with the cream in a bowl. Season with salt and pepper.
2. Melt the butter in a large (if possible, nonstick) frying pan until it gently sizzles. Pour in the egg mixture and cook over a moderately low heat, stirring continuously, until cooked, about six to seven minutes. The eggs should have a creamy, smooth, scrambled-egg appearance.
3. Transfer the egg dip to a serving bowl and sprinkle with the chopped chives. Serve with the cooked cocktail sausages, bacon strips, small rolled-up slices of smoked salmon, tomato wedges, toast and crusty bread. Enjoy while warm.

Garlic Dip

MAKES ABOUT 300 ML/10 FL OZ

The base for this dip is home-made mayonnaise, which can be used in any of the other recipes requiring mayonnaise. However, if you are concerned about eating raw eggs, then use ready-made mayonnaise, made from pasteurized eggs. As ever, the secret to making a successful mayonnaise is patience – add the oil very gradually and beat each addition in well before adding any more. If the oil is added too quickly, it will fail to emulsify and the mixture will separate. Using a blender or food processor has taken all the hard work out of beating the oil in by hand.

2 egg yolks
½ tsp salt
¼ tsp mustard powder
¼ tsp ground white pepper
¼ tsp caster sugar
125 ml/4 fl oz olive oil
125 ml/4 fl oz sunflower oil
1 Tbsp lemon juice·
4 garlic cloves, crushed
Strips of carrot, celery, cucumber and peppers;
small broccoli and cauliflower florets

1. Place the egg yolks, salt, mustard, pepper and sugar in a blender or food processor and blend on high speed for about fifteen seconds.
2. Reduce the speed to medium and initially add the oil, drop by drop, through the hole in the lid. As the oil is blended into the egg yolks, very slowly drizzle the oil into the mixture, blending until a smooth mayonnaise has been made. Add the lemon juice and garlic then transfer to a bowl, cover and chill.

3. Spoon the dip into a serving bowl and surround with strips of carrot, celery, cucumber and peppers, and small florets of broccoli and cauliflower.

Tahini Dip

MAKES ABOUT 300 ML/10 FL OZ

Tahini is made from sesame seeds and has a very distinctive flavour. Although this dip looks very thin when first made, once chilled it thickens to a good dipping consistency.

50 g/2 oz light tahini
150 g/5 oz natural yogurt
50 ml/2 fl oz unsweetened apple juice
1 tsp cider vinegar
1 garlic clove, crushed (optional)
Freshly ground black pepper
Cored apple wedges, strips of celery and crisps

1. Soften the tahini in a bowl with a spoon so that the yogurt will blend in more readily. Add the yogurt and mix well.
2. Stir in the apple juice, cider vinegar and garlic, if using. Season well with freshly ground black pepper to taste. Cover and chill.
3. Spoon the dip into a serving dish and serve with cored apple wedges (dipped in lemon juice to prevent discolouring), strips of celery and potato crisps.

WHAT GOES WITH WHAT

WHAT GOES WITH WHAT

The charts here and on the following pages show at a glance the variety of dips and the accompaniments well suited to them as dipping foods. Feel free to experiment. The chart can be used as inspiration for other serving ideas.

CHEESE DIPS	ACCOMPANIMENTS				
	VEGETABLE	FRUIT	SEAFOOD	BREADS	SNACKS
Beer and Cheddar Dip	trimmed spring onions			breadsticks	potato crisps
Blue Cheese Dip	celery strips, florets of cauliflower and broccoli				
Brie and Pear Dip		small wedges of cantaloupe and watermelon			
Cheese and Pimento Dip				breadsticks	tortilla and potato crisps
Cottage Cheese and Caper Dip	strips of red, green, yellow peppers, raddichio leaves		fish sticks		
Cream Cheese and Chive Dip	red onion wedges, celery, carrot and pepper strips				
Dill, Yogurt, and Cream Cheese Dip	fennel, endive, cucumber strips		fish sticks		
Edam Dip	quartered button mushrooms, tomato wedges, broccoli florets, carrot strips				
Green Olive and Cream Cheese Dip				breadsticks, warm pitta bread strips	
Mountain High Dip	celery, cucumber, carrot strips			chunks of crusty bread	
Peppercorn Cheese Dip	cucumber and carrot strips			breadsticks	cheese straws
Pistachio and Blue Cheese Dip	celery strips	cored apple wedges		crusty bread	
Ricotta and Cream Walnut Dip	celery strips	cored apple wedges		cubed bagels	
Smoked Cheese Dip	tomato wedges, cucumber strips			toasted cubed bread	crackers

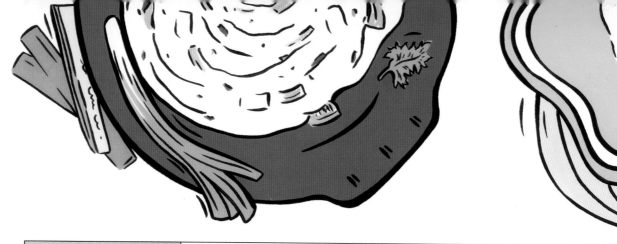

FISH DIPS	ACCOMPANIMENTS			
	VEGETABLE	SEAFOOD	BREAD	SNACKS
Avocado and Tuna Dip	courgette and carrot strips, blanched green beans			cheese straws
Bagna Cauda	fennel, celery, carrot strips		cubed crusty bread	
Caper and Tartare Dip	strips of peppers, crisp lettuce leaves	fish sticks		
Chive and Smoked Oyster Dip			melba toast	
Crab Dip				potato crisps, salty snacks
Creamy Caviar Dip			melba toast	
Creamy Tuna Dip	celery and cucumber strips, baby sweet corn, tomato wedges			
Devilled Egg and Tuna Dip	celery strips		toasted garlic bread	tortilla crisps
Prawn Cocktail Dip	crisp lettuce leaves, celery and cucumber strips		melba toast	
Quick Anchovy Dip	green and black olives, quartered button mushrooms, pepper strips		chunks of Ciabatta or olive bread	
Smoked Mackerel and Horseradish Dip			toasted triangles of white and brown bread	
Smoked Salmon and Lemon Dip	cucumber, celery, carrot strips		melba toast	
Taramasalata			warm pitta bread strips	
Thai Coconut and Chilli Crab Dip	trimmed spring onions, strips of red pepper, cucumber, carrot			rice and prawn crackers

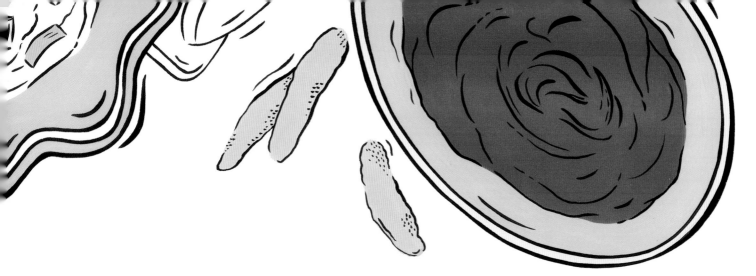

MEAT DIPS	ACCOMPANIMENTS				
	VEGETABLE	FRUIT	MEAT	BREAD	SNACKS
Beef and Creamed Horseradish Dip	tomato wedges, crisp lettuce leaves, French fries				
Chicken and Almond Dip	cucumber, carrot, peppers, courgette strips			cubed bagels or crusty bread	
Chicken Liver and Mushroom Dip				melba toast, rye bread	crackers
Chorizo Sausage and Tomato Dip				chunks of crusty bread or garlic bread	
Ham and Gruyère Dip	cucumber, celery and carrot strips				
Peanut Satay Style Dip	cucumber and pepper strips, trimmed spring onions		stir-fried pork strips – see recipe on page 27		
Quick Tangy Tomato Dip	French fries, celery, cucumber, courgette strips		batter-coated turkey dipping sticks – see recipe on page 28		
Roasted Peanut and Ham Dip	celery, cucumber and carrot strips, tomato wedges			breadsticks	potato crisps, crackers
Smoked Ham and Pineapple Dip		wedges of mango, paw-paw, melon			
Smoky Bacon and Cream Cheese Dip	celery strips			breadsticks	selection of crackers

VEGETABLE DIPS	ACCOMPANIMENTS				
	VEGETABLE	SEAFOOD	MEAT	BREAD	SNACKS
Artichoke Heart Dip	grilled vegetables, e.g. red and yellow pepper, courgettes and aubergine strips				
Asparagus Cream Dip	chilled, cooked young asparagus tips and green beans; endive				
Aubergine and Pepper Dip				warm slices of crusty garlic bread	
Black Olive Dip				wedges of olive bread or Ciabatta	
Butternut Squash Dip	fried or oven-roasted sweet potato wedges				
Celery and Spinach Dip					selection of small cheese crackers
Creamy Corn Dip	cucumber, carrot, celery strips			cubed bagels	cheese straws
Cucumber and Lime Riata	cucumber and celery strips			warm pitta bread strips, crusty bread	
Guacamole	pepper strips				tortilla crisps
Mushroom and Pine Nut Dip				strips of crusty bread	selection of crackers
Puréed Vegetable and Pumpkin Seed Dip				wedges of breads, e.g. Ciabatta, tomato, olive, pumpernickel	
Quick and Easy BBQ Dip	and green peppers	BBQ or grilled quarters of yellow	chicken drumsticks, spare ribs and sausages		BBQ or grilled
Radish Dip	crisp lettuce leaves, cucumber and celery strips	cooked, peeled jumbo prawns			

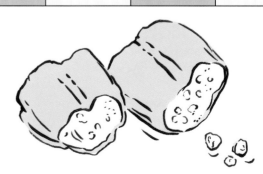

VEGETABLE DIPS	ACCOMPANIMENTS (CONTINUED)				
	VEGETABLE	SEAFOOD	MEAT	BREAD	SNACKS
Scarlet Delight Dip	fennel, celery, courgettes, cucumber strips				
Sesame and Red Pepper Dip	blanched and chilled mange tout, baby sweet corn; celery and cucumber strips				rice and prawn crackers
Smooth Chilli Tomato Dip	deep-fried batter-coated vegetables (e.g. onion rings, cauliflower and broccoli florets), pepper strips	cooked, peeled jumbo prawns		pitta bread strips	
Spring Onion Dip	crisp lettuce leaves, courgettes and pepper strips				potato crisps
Sun-dried Tomato Stunner Dip	yellow, orange, red, green pepper strips			warm garlic bread	
Sweet and Sour Dip	celery, cucumber, carrot, yellow and red pepper strips, canned water chestnuts, blanched and chilled baby sweet corn and mange tout				prawn crackers
Tapenade				toasted crusty bread, olive bread	
Tomato and Basil Dip	cucumber, celery, courgette strips			breadsticks	
Tomato and Chilli Salsa	wide strips of red, yellow, green, orange peppers				tortilla crisps
Tomato and Onion Sambal				pitta bread strips	
Tzatziki	pan-fried strips of courgettes				
Watercress and Yogurt Dip	crisp small lettuce leaves, celery and carrot strips	cooked crumb- or batter-coated salmon or white fish sticks			

BEAN AND LENTIL DIPS	ACCOMPANIMENTS				
	VEGETABLE	FRUIT	SEAFOOD	BREAD	SNACKS
Butter Bean Dip	carrot strips, broccoli florets, blanched green beans		fish sticks or scampi		
Creamed Chickpea and Hazelnut Dip	celery and cucumber strips	cored apple wedges			potato crisps
Curried Bean Dip				pitta bread strips, crusty bread	
Green Lentil and Spinach Dip	pepper strips			pitta bread strips	
Hot Tex Mex Dip	pepper strips				tortilla crisps, taco shells
Hummus	peppers, celery, cucumber strips			pitta bread strips	
Mexican Bean Dip	red, yellow, green pepper strips				tortilla crisps
Pesto Bean Dip	tomato wedges			breadsticks, cubed crusty bread, olive bread	
Red Lentil Dhal	celery and cucumber strips			warm strips of pitta bread, crusty bread	

SAVOURY FRUIT DIPS	ACCOMPANIMENTS					
	VEGETABLE	FRUIT	MEAT	BREAD	SNACKS	SWEETS
Apricot and Mango Chutney Dip	onion rings			crusty bread	samosas	
Cranberry and Orange Dip			crumb-coated turkey sticks – see page 52			
Curried Mango Dip	cucumber, red pepper strips			pitta bread strips, crusty bread		
Paw-paw, Mango and Pomegranate Salsa	wide strips of red, yellow, green peppers				tortilla crisps	
Pineapple, Avocado and Red Onion Salsa				pitta bread strips	tortilla crisps, nachos	
Pineapple and Chive Cheese Dip	celery, cucumber, carrot strips				selection of crackers	

SWEET FRUIT DIPS	ACCOMPANIMENTS					
	VEGETABLE	FRUIT	MEAT	BREAD	SNACKS	SWEETS
Autumnal Fruits with Port Dip		cored apple wedges				mini sweet muffins, sponge fingers, marshmallows
Blueberry Swirl Dip		cored pear wedges				chocolate and vanilla cake
Butterscotch Dip		grilled bananas – see page 58				
Cinnamon and Raisin Yogurt Dip		apple fritters – see recipe on page 57				
Kiwi Cream Dip		wedges of mango, paw-paw, banana				
Strawberry Dream Dip		wedges of pear, peach, banana				marshmallows, mini doughnuts, mini sweet muffins

MORE FAVOURITES	ACCOMPANIMENTS					
	VEGETABLE	FRUIT	SEAFOOD	MEAT	BREAD	SNACKS
Caper and Gherkin Dip	red, yellow, green pepper, courgette and celery strips					
Creamy Egg Brunch Dip	tomato wedges		sliced smoked salmon rolled up into bite-sized pieces	cooked cocktail sausages, grilled smoked bacon strips	toast and crusty bread	
Egg and Parsley Dip					strips of white and brown toast	
Fresh Herbed Yogurt Dip	vegetable kebabs, strips of raw vegetables		fish kebabs	meat kebabs		
Garlic Dip	carrot, celery, pepper strips, broccoli and cauliflower florets					
Peppery Mayonnaise Dip	celery, carrot, cucumber, courgette strips; blanched baby sweet corn					
Tahini Dip	celery strips	cored apple wedges				potato crisps
Tofu and Peanut Butter Dip	strips of peppers				toasted bread strips	
Tofu and Sesame Dip	celery, cucumber, peppers, carrot strips, broccoli and cauliflower florets					
Wholegrain Mustard Dip	deep-fried baked batter-coated vegetables, e.g. onion rings, strips of aubergine and courgette					

FONDUES	ACCOMPANIMENTS					
	VEGETABLE	FRUIT	SEAFOOD	MEAT	BREAD	SWEETS
Cider and Cheese Fondue	cucumber and celery chunks, tomato wedges	cored apple wedges		strips of cooked ham	cubed crusty bread	
Creamy Toffee Fondue						plain popcorn
Devil's Chocolate Fondue						cubed sponge cake, mini sweet muffins, mini doughnuts, biscuits
Double Cheese Fondue	diced peppers, tomato wedges, sliced courgettes				cubed crusty bread, small breadsticks, cheese straws	
Fresh Tomato and Basil Fondue	diced peppers, celery chunks		shelled cooked jumbo prawns		cubed crusty bread and garlic bread	
Marshmallow Delight Fondue		seedless grapes, sliced banana and peaches, strawberries				

A

Apricot and Mango Chutney Dip 53
Artichoke Heart Dip 42
Asparagus Cream Dip 41
Aubergine and Pepper Dip 40
Autumnal Fruits with Port Dip 58
Avocado and Tuna Dip 23

B

Bagna Cauda 24
Beef and Creamed Horseradish Dip 31
Beer and Cheddar Dip 13
Black Olive Dip 34
Blueberry Swirl Dip 56
Blue Cheese Dip 18
Brie and Pear Dip 15
Butter Bean Dip 49
Butternut Squash Dip 44
Butterscotch Dip with Grilled Bananas 58

C

Caper and Gherkin Dip 65
Caper and Tartare Dip 20
Celery and Spinach Dip 42
Cheese and Pimento Dip 14
Chicken and Almond Dip 32
Chicken Liver and Mushroom Dip 32
Chive and Smoked Oyster Dip 23
Chorizo Sausage and Tomato Dip 31
Cider and Cheese Fondue 60
Cinnamon and Raisin Yogurt Dip with Apple Fritters 57
Cottage Cheese and Caper Dip 18
Crab Dip 25
Cranberry and Orange Dip with Herbed Crumb-coated Turkey Sticks 52–3
Cream Cheese and Chive Dip 17
Creamed Chickpea and Hazelnut Dip 50
Creamy Caviar Dip 20
Creamy Corn Dip 45
Creamy Egg Brunch Dip 68
Creamy Toffee Fondue with Popcorn 62
Creamy Tuna Dip 21
Cucumber and Lime Raita 45

Curried Bean Dip 49
Curried Mango Dip 55

D

Devilled Egg and Tuna Dip 23
Devil's Chocolate Fondue 63
Dill, Yogurt and Cream Cheese Dip 16
Double Cheese Fondue 61

E

Edam Dip 18
Egg and Parsley Dip 66

F

Fresh Herbed Yogurt Dip 66
Fresh Tomato and Basil Fondue 62

G

Garlic Dip 69
Green Lentil and Spinach Dip 49
Green Olive and Cream Cheese Dip 13
Guacamole 39

H

Ham and Gruyère Dip 29
Hot Tex Mex Dip 48
Hummus 47

K

Kiwi Cream Dip 56

M

Marshmallow Delight Fondue 63
Mexican Bean Dip 50
Mountain High Dip 17
Mushroom and Pine Nut Dip 44

P

Paw-paw, Mango and Pomegranate Salsa 55
Peanut Satay Style Dip with Stir-Fried Pork Strips 27
Peppercorn Cheese Dip 16
Peppery Mayonnaise Dip 65
Pesto Bean Dip 50
Pineapple and Chive Cheese Dip 54
Pineapple, Avocado and Red Onion Salsa 53

Pistachio and Blue Cheese Dip 15
Prawn Cocktail Dip 25
Puréed Vegetable and Pumpkin Seed Dip 38

Q

Quick Anchovy Dip 20
Quick and Easy BBQ Dip 39
Quick Tangy Tomato Dip with Turkey Dipping Sticks 28–9

R

Radish Dip 36
Red Lentil Dhal 47
Ricotta and Cream Walnut Dip 13
Roasted Peanut and Ham Dip 31

S

Scarlet Delight Dip 35
Sesame and Red Pepper Dip 41
Smoked Cheese Dip 15
Smoked Ham and Pineapple Dip 30
Smoked Mackerel and Horseradish Dip 21
Smoked Salmon and Lemon Dip 21
Smoky Bacon and Cream Cheese Dip 29
Smooth Chilli Tomato Dip 40
Spring Onion Dip 36
Strawberry Dream Dip 56
Sun-dried Tomato Stunner Dip 37
Sweet and Sour Dip with Chinese Vegetables 36

T

Tahini Dip 69
Tapenade 45
Taramasalata 24
Thai Coconut and Chilli Crab Dip 22
Tofu and Peanut Butter Dip 67
Tofu and Sesame Dip 67
Tomato and Basil Dip 37
Tomato and Chilli Salsa 43
Tomato and Onion Sambal 42
Tzatziki 34

W

Watercress and Yogurt 34
Wholegrain Mustard Dip 65